EMBLEMS OF FREEDOM

A JOURNEY THROUGH GLACIER & YELLOWSTONE NATIONAL PARKS

BY
CRAIG LEIBFREID

COVER ART BY TAYLOR LAMBERT

Printed in the United States of America

ISBN 979-8-89114-063-9 (sc)
ISBN 979-8-89114-064-6 (e)

Library of Congress Control Number: 2024902514

2024.04.05

MainSpring Books
5901 W. Century Blvd
Suite 750
Los Angeles, CA, US, 90045

www.mainspringbooks.com

FOREWORD

On Tyranny

Tyranny and fascism can have multiple origins. Where they lead is toward an imbalance of authority. What they do not propagate is balance. Without balance there is no harmony. Without harmony there is no peace. Peace, harmony, and understanding are emblematic of the free world where we have the liberty to express our nature, and share in a loving relationship with God. Dark energy in fascism and tyranny outweighs light energy. It could be greed, a grudge, bitterness, thirst for power, among other things that do not offer peace. They belittle tolerance; peaceful communication between people with differing ideas. Whatever it is, fascism and tyranny are things unholy and selfish. If we are to have convictions, may they be holy and for the goodness of the world. It is not likely that hatred is felt and identified by fascist tyrants. They are detached from those they rule over. Freedoms for the people are necessary to express justice, and being a peacemaker does not mean sitting idly by while injustice is happening around you. Freedom must be protected. When no one is defending freedom, when no one is practicing communion with the spirit of goodness, when no one is making sacrifices, fascists gain momentum. Freedom is vigilant and outspoken. Peace is tranquil. Despite subtle differences, peace and freedom are complementary. I'm not sure if sociopaths have a soft enough heart to understand what hatred is. I don't think they take the time to reflect on what they're living out. I don't think they fully consider justice, morality, and the directive of peacemakers. If fascists do feel hatred, it appears they embrace it, and it only fuels the fire of warfare. The atrocities committed by fascists onto their victims is probably seen as something acceptable, negotiable, and even innocent or humorous by *their* perception. This is a perspective issue. Delusions fill the mind, and they ignore harmony. They are dishonest and compromise any truth that might have existed within them. A pampered life leaves *little* room for feelings of sympathy towards hardship. If you haven't experienced hardship, you probably won't be able to show compassion for those facing their trials. If you can sympathize with those at the other end of the spectrum, then you have realized the compassion of Christ, but sympathy alone is not embracing justice. To embrace justice, we must put love into action. For those who don't put love into action and embrace our differences through equality, the desire for authority drives them to destroy the good of the world for the sake of their ego. The Bible claims the Devil rules over the Earth, and the only way to claim authority over the evil of this world is through Jesus. Compassion and altruism fail to live in the heart of tyrants. If the fruit of their actions is not fair and honest, what grounds of justification do they have? Maybe fascists take pride in how nasty they can be towards other people, as if their wrath is something to be admired or respected. The greed for power might be embedded within the ability to destroy something beautiful, disrupt harmony, and turn fear and awe towards oneself. The desire to destroy beauty only exists within an oversized ego. Nastiness and tyranny might invoke fear, but respect is something fascism shall not warrant.

Emblems of Freedom

In the age of a heavy world
We ran headlong against the wind
Poverty, war, sickness
Chaos, will it end?

Rails spanning a continent
We boarded the train
Minds burdened,
Who shall remain?

Not by fear, but rather curiosity
We set out on an adventure
In pursuit of truth
Our minds they could not censure

To connect, to commune
With spirits Holy, could we be immune?
Products of the environment
Tyranny will not stand.
Let peace and restoration be thy command.

INTRODUCTION

The Russian-Ukrainian war and the Covid-19 pandemic among other great perils of the early 21st century weighed heavy on many peopled, and the fallout felt endless. As it is said, "all things shall pass." There must be a way out. As divine timing would have it, my wife Kelly and I would take a great outdoor adventure to Glacier and Yellowstone National Parks in August of 2022. It felt like a way out, and an opportunity to reflect on solutions. Here I share our experience and what it taught us; an override from the fear by way of freedom and justice. It revealed age-old, universal truths that could restore harmony, harmony being active or passive, but it must work toward bringing peace to the greater good. There must be a way to communicate peacefully. America needs to be a free and peaceful state. After all, the true aim of tolerance is for everyone, will all our different views, to communicate peaceably. But what is emblematic of freedom? Tyranny felt like it was spreading like wildfire at the time. Lots of people were hungry for power, but Kelly and I were searching for balance. Understandably, our experience and this account of it cannot solve the world's problems, but, in part, it did bring us peace. Everyone needs to connect with the world that surrounds us, and we should all be reminded that we are accountable for the lives we live here on Earth. There is more to life than what we see in this world. Promoting the greater good in order to sustain harmonious relationships needs focus. Submitting to a higher power in a relationship with God is the best way to ensure positive accountability. Harmonious relationships ride on respect. Respect, universal respect, is mandatory for we all have been made in the image of the love and strength of God. That is a universal truth.

Universal truth was something that became bolder in my mind through the trip. I was searching for answers, and the natural world always seemed to provide them. Through communion I could see things that were steadfast and supported by the miracle of nature and transcendental experience. Things like being honest and fair, having a good heart attitude towards God, and inherently being made in God's image of love and strength pervaded my mind as things that could not be ignored nor ever disproved. God created. Jesus is messiah. We are all sinners. That might have been the outcome of the bits that pieced together along the way, each day shining a brilliance that came from reaching the high altitudes of Glacier and Yellowstone. Our problems came some from somewhere along the course of time. They didn't just magically appear. There were mechanics to it. There is much distaste for the church and Christianity, but I think the bigger problem is world leaders who choose to ignore God, and societies that encourage the culture to do the same. This decade has pushed us into a storm that most of the people alive on Earth have not experienced. 1st world countries might be seeing the hardships that have existed in the world all along, but the American people and most of the western world have been pushed into a state of fear and hostility that has destabilized society and communities to a point that you cannot rely on people for any amount of goodness. Admittedly, though, through our hardships we have come together and grown stronger, but it seems the adversary we are fighting has gotten bolder too. Division feels stronger, and the media and government are trying to steer the narrative away from a government of the people, by the people, and for the people. I will believe in God and that good will prevail. This too shall pass.

PART I

A Journey Through Glacier and Yellowstone National Parks

CHAPTER 1

Train from Pennsylvania to Montana

We left Johnstown, Pennsylvania on a rainy Sunday evening in July 2022. It was the last day of the month. The steel town of the 1970's & 80's has been revitalized. Luckily there was always an Amtrak station in town. The Stonycreek River and Little Conemaugh River valleys converged in the city to form the Conemaugh River flowing toward the west, the direction the train would take us. Valley walls rose green about 1,000ft in every direction. The mountains east of Pittsburgh divided the Chesapeake Bay and Ohio River drainages. Our train was two hours late. We were headed west, Whitefish, Montana to be exact. There was joy in the journey; spirits driven by adventure and discovery. When traveling, we are ever mindful of the destination. Unanticipated treasures along the way give deeper meaning to the adventure. When the things you don't expect to find overcome you, you are amazed. Kelly and I hoped to find harmony, vision, anything transcendental on this 3-week trip. The world was a mess, and we were looking for truth, restoration, and a little escape. We left the Appalachian Mtns. of Pennsylvania headed for Glacier and Yellowstone National Parks by train Sunday July 31, 2022. We would rent a car and roam Montana and Wyoming until August 19, 2022. In that search for epiphany, I had an advantage: no preconceived conceptions. I had some fears. Car breaking down in remote places. Running into bears. Train hiccups. Before our trip I was nervous about the layovers in Chicago and Pittsburgh. Despite a few close calls, nothing terrible happened on the trip. I got myself nervous leading up to the endeavor but could do nothing about the future until it became the present. I was stepping out of my comfort zone, but I would live in the moment, and negotiate the problems as they came. The first step was finding harmony. Harmony, even as an internal sense, requires a measure of patience, patience to move in time with your surroundings.

After much anticipation, we were at the Johnstown Amtrak station Sunday evening waiting for our train to arrive. As I stood in front of the old building, I had a feeling of nostalgia. It was a sleepy kind of Sunday evening, grey skies, light rain. I peered out into the dampness and city landscape. The environment before me reminded me of other times I had slipped away from Johnstown to explore distant regions of the world. It was the ability to disconnect and find something a little more primal; peace and open-mindedness. There felt like so much division in the world at that time that I hoped by some strange stroke of luck this trip would capture some unity. The train was running two hours behind, but we passed the time patiently. For a three-week trip, a few hours' delay in the beginning was nothing to get hung up on. Still, an uneasy start to the adventure. We finally boarded our train around 8:00 PM. We dropped our bags off in coach and found our way to the café car. Kelly and I each had an IPA and split a chicken bacon ranch wrap. We would certainly eat good on the trip, but improvising for meals became something of a habit on the adventure. It was just enough food and beer to keep us from getting hungry for the next few hours. It wasn't much in the way to fill us up, but we were taking in the calories where we could get them.

A little before 10:00 PM the train pulled into Pittsburgh. We grabbed our backpacks and 2 large totes. Her camera equipment was in one, and tent, sleeping bags, and percolator for coffee in the other. The tote bags looked like lumpy suitcases. With lumpy suitcases in hand, we walked from the train station to Market Square where we had beers at the "City Works." The jaunt to the bar had me reeling in a July-evening-feel. It was warm, dark, and humid. Something felt very free and a little bold. Walking the streets that night was liberating. It felt like there was little in the way of responsibility, but much in the way of possibility in the balmy evening air.

We arrived at "City Works" and stashed our bags near the door, then Kelly and I took seats at the bar and ordered some beer. We each got a pint of a Helles Lager. We didn't linger around long, but I had a second beer, a dunkel, before we left. It felt a little contrived, pounding beers on a Sunday night while waiting only two hours for trains to connect. We got back to the train station by 11:30, and didn't have to wait long to board the midnight train to Chicago. We passed through the station, and walked down the platform. The train stretched a few hundred yards, car linked to car, silver with a blue stripe, and standing about 15 feet tall. There was something kind of stoic and omnipotent about the appearance of the train from out on the platform. It was so large and ominous that it just kind of shouted, "Yeah. I'm gonna take you to your destination." We got to our car and boarded. We had a sleeper cabin, and crawled into bed after getting on the train and finding our room. I was asleep pretty quickly and only woke once through the night somewhere close to Cleveland, Ohio. I couldn't see much out of the top bunk, but it wasn't a bother. The bed was up close against the ceiling of the railcar, and it was a little challenging for a 6'2" 190 lb. man to get situated and comfortable. Kelly and I woke around sunrise. She had a terrible migraine that morning and was vomiting into a shopping bag as we rode into Chicago. Anytime she gets sick, I feel bad. I feel like there is next to nothing I can do to make her feel better. Helplessness before a loved one in discomfort is a painful feeling. It was a pretty bad way to start the 20-day trip, and I was trying to conceptualize how this problem would evolve. My only hope was that it would quickly resolve itself.

We were rolling through the Midwest that morning. The landscape was not the most intriguing. It appeared to be a series of farm-fields, swamps, and factories, in that order, repeating itself every so many miles. The Midwest was a bit different than the Appalachian Mountains. There didn't look to be much of anything inspiring in the landscape of northern Ohio, and northern Indiana. There appeared to be little escape from the world of capitalism and commerce, maybe four-wheelers and hunting whitetails; rural communities without much mystery in the landscape. There was no place to hide from the farm fields and chemical plants. It lacked variety. We arrived at the Chicago train station around 9:00 AM. Kelly was struggling to feel any level of comfort, and I was a little dazed from the train ride myself. I didn't sleep great in our railcar. We got off at the train station and walked out to the patio along the Chicago River. Amidst the landscape of skyscrapers we were in a bit of a greenspace with wide sidewalks stretching for blocks to only accommodate foot traffic. The Chicago River was recessed 20 feet below the sidewalk. Corporate buildings filled the city blocks and benches were located beneath moderate tree cover between the walkways. Lots of foot traffic passed by in the handsome American city. Smiles, sunglasses, and pretty faces. There was a lot of tobacco pinched that morning. I didn't want to get too engaged with anyone or anything for that glimpse of time that we spent waiting for our 3:05 train to Montana. Kelly's discomfort had me preoccupied. I was also trying to maintain patience as we had five hours to kill until our next train departed. The pigeons were being rude. As we tried to warm up to them, we made one extremely uncomfortable and a little self-conscious by pointing at it and talking about it. I was doing my best to try to ease Kelly out of her migraine, but the situation just had to run its course. Time had to pass and there was little I could do for her. We bought lunch from a Chic-Fil-A in the train station, and continued to wait for our connecting line.

Like I said, we were on the hunt for something transcendental. It found us pretty quick. Along the foot street on the Chicago River, a man passed by the name of Jason. He was a white male about 45 years old. He was clean cut, and it started with a comment about our bags. He was carrying an army surplus backpack, and spotted our hand-sewn, lumpy suitcase with fabric of tribal, psychedelic design colored in earthy tones. Jason's remark was something to the effect that rarely does he see people carrying more bags than him. Maybe our appearance was attractive: a minimalist carry-on, hip dress, long hair, and sunglasses. We struck up a conversation as Kelly and I continued to wait for the train. I found out this man quit his job, sold his apartment and roamed the streets for the past few months or years. He was a bit of a mystic. We talked about the state of the world from a spiritual standpoint. He explained to me how he received and exorcism in prison, and became born again, and later baptized. He claimed to be Jewish (yet received a Christian baptism). We talked about the continuum of time and the possibility of the world being in the midst of rapture. Jason stated rapture would last 7 years, while I was of the mind it would take 3 ½ years. Jason explained his disposition on the war between good and evil, and how there are now more angels than demons in the world. He thought that much of the world would not be saved upon its final judgment. Too much empty living by too many empty people. Their loss is not my fault, and I simply can't be everyone's reason for coming into a relationship with God no matter how many of my books I try to share with people or how many times I engage in gospel conversations. We talked about balancing light and dark energy; spirit. I was of the mind that we should always be a light in the darkness. Jason suggested I should carry a little more-dark energy to keep balance in such a depraved world. He said I carried a lot of light, and I needed a little more dark. He called me a star-seed, and later found out it's a term to define someone who originated on another planet or galaxy. The idea is a little abstract, maybe obscure to some, but a few of us might not have been meant for this world. Conceptualized elsewhere, and serving a purpose to the world, not absorbing its ways. Is it possible for souls to originate in different dimensions? Sent to this dimension for the sake of the Lord's work, but not to remain in this dimension, here on Earth, or have worldly things living in them? We can only speculate, but I believe there is more to life than what we see in this world.

After a long day at the Chicago train station, we anxiously boarded the Empire Builder line on Amtrak that would take us all the way to Whitefish, MT. Boarding a train in a train station is kind of a sight and an experience, especially in Chicago. The train paddock is sometimes dark and closed off from the rest of the world. Droves of people marching through the darkness with bags in hand towards the ominous railcars, diesel engines humming in the background. We got on the train, into another sleeper, where Kelly and I would spend the next 31 hours. We started rolling out around 4:00 PM on a sunny August 1st. Once on the train, it took us a little while to get out of urban Illinois, but as we worked our way beyond the city of Milwaukee, and into rural Wisconsin, the sun was setting over the fields in the beautiful August evening. The landscape there was more dynamic than I predicted. Green topography rose and fell, and even exhibited a few rocky bluffs. The vegetation reminded me of the lowlands of Norway. The Great Lakes region of the Upper Midwest was inspiring peace and intrigue. There was a subtle beauty as I peered on in majesty out the window onto the comfortable rural communities of Wisconsin.

At 5:30 we went to the dining car, where, by luck, we ate with a mother and daughter. Amanda, the daughter, looked to be in her mid-20's, and Cathy, the mother, looked to be in her late 50's. They were from Minneapolis, returning home from the alt-rock music festival, Lollapalooza, in Chicago the weekend prior. They weren't terribly hip, trendy, or counter-culture, but Kelly and I shared some nice conversation with them over dinner about culture in Minnesota and Western PA. It focused around heritage, college sports, and the occupations people hold within their communities. We talked about the Scandinavian heritage of the upper Midwest and Eastern European heritage of western Pennsylvania and how those things affect dialects spoken in such regions. We moved on to college sports: hockey, football, wrestling, and Penn State University and the University of Minnesota, both Big Ten Conference colleges. The following for those two sports teams turn the regions and their communities into fanatics, whether it is tailgating, or games being played over radio in grocery stores. Not something I'm terribly proud of but an unignorable fact in certain places. Culture and its influences are dynamic that way. The relations we hold with the entities around us, how they move and inspire us, affects the way we interact with others outside of those entities. That is why it is important for the institutions of the world not to live in us. Culture is an expression of the institutions, achievements, and follies of a people. Those institutions are affected by everything we come in contact with, and different from place to place. Variety in that is not only amusing or entertaining but has the ability to enrich the greater scope of our world, and also has the ability to cripple us. Though enrichment depends on our values. Just as they can enrich, they can detract from the quality of the world. Institutions, whether they be our work space, preferred form of entertainment, or social groups should not coax us to be boastful, bossy, or arrogant. They should not create division. Dinner conversation wrapped up over whitewater river festivals and music festivals. The food on the Empire Builder was astounding, the first good meal I had in over a day, and what a meal it was!

We returned from dinner to our sleeper around 6:45. We peered through the window from the seats in our room over the green-gold of the countryside. The sun was setting in that hazy August evening way. Soft light and intense heat could be sensed just outside the windows of the train. We crossed the Mississippi River in LaCrosse, Wisconsin around sunset. The largest river in the country was a stark contrast from its mouth in bayou country. We were in the north woods as we crossed near the source of 'Big Muddy' that evening. The Mississippi was kind of surreal. Evening twilight in such a watershed held auras of something very middle America that was not quite traditional or dogmatic. The expression of spirit embodied in the landscape at that place, at that time, felt pristine and a little mysterious. Freedom could be sensed. A detachment from the institutions of society filled that broad valley. And the train kept rolling. As evening turned to the dark of night, the spirit of those moments stuck with me.

There was always something special about water meeting sky around twilight. A nice balance of light and dark. It reminded me of Jason from Chicago. That balance is a method of finding harmony, but I think harmony is more than that. On the most intimate level, harmony is found in synchronizing different wavelengths. When energy from one body moves at a particular wavelength and frequency, all bodies that wish to move in time with it must move at the same wavelength and frequency. They must harmonize. That takes good communication. Harmonizing light and dark and harmonizing varying wavelengths might be more similar than I'm willing to admit. We ought to be realistic in our definitions about contrast and harmony although our definitions of those things don't have to be put at opposite ends of the spectrum where it creates division. One, the other, or maybe both allow for a measure of dark to exist amongst light for the sake of balance. Still, it's hard to communicate to one end of the spectrum from the other about tolerance and cooperation. You got to find a little middle ground and make a compromise from where you are to where you want to be. You cannot change without actually *making* that change. Finding balance takes an element of mysticism. Stepping out from where you are to pursue where you want to be cannot thoroughly be predicted or forecasted without experience. There will be the unexpected as the change progresses. Change requires us to look deeper at things and make sacrifices to bring about harmony between ourselves and our environment. If we ourselves want to harmonize with other bodies, we must understand the internal composition and habit of those things.

Most institutions of society would prefer for us to believe harmony is a rather heretic concept, and unachievable without buying into their dogma. Admittedly, it is hard to feel a sense of community and belonging when you always feel in danger in your home. But tolerance is a mechanism to promote peaceable communication. Support and validation begin with respect. God asks us to respect everyone for we are all made in His image of love and strength. Humanity has been working to harmonize for a long time. Look at Dr. Martin Luther King Jr. and the civil rights movement of the 1960's. Current progressives would like you to believe that real changes have not been made by him and his fellows. Real progress has been made. A higher level of harmony between different races and classes now exists. But some don't want to acknowledge that progress. Some want to hang their hat on unrealistic, self-deprecating philosophies. Division and tribalism draws in more money than togetherness and real solutions. How can we possibly listen to someone we disagree with? Soften your heart and let your ear do more work than your mouth. That's how. Why should I sacrifice my personal truth for the sake of universal truth? The answer is that universal truth provides more harmony with making fewer sacrifices for the greater good.

The next day I woke up on the train in North Dakota. The sunrise was beautiful. The way morning twilight sprawled across the landscape hearkened the soul. It was something unfamiliar but ever so reverent. It was not something I knew well, the High Plains, but it was so integral to everything, or at least half of everything this country represents. I've never seen such flat dry land, quite desolate, but still holding life. I'm not sure what captured my attention the most. Maybe it was the saturation of farmland and low population density. Maybe it was the topography or lack there-of. Maybe it was the weather on the High Plains at that time of year. Kelly and I were trying to remove ourselves from society, and find a little restoration for the soul. A train ride through North Dakota might count as that. Already, we could feel a mend on balance in the interpersonal as well as introspective battles in our lives. Desolation allows us time to reflect, and better understand truth. Maybe we don't give ourselves enough time to reflect on life to rightly understand truth. Truth and balance can be seen in a spectrum of light and dark. It can be binary. It can be yes and no; black or white; on or off. But also, the relationships we hold between ourselves and the natural world around us harmonizes in wavelengths. It's more qualitative than quantitative. With all that in mind, all must be rooted in universal truth and not personal truth or else we will get lost in a life framed in by delusions.

I was getting lost in the northern prairie; flat, glaciated by continental glaciers. The land was vast. Line of sight stretched for miles. The breath of land that could be seen by the eye let the imagination expand. Possibilities seemed infinite. Along the landscape, there were eskers, lakes, and dark rich soil. There weren't a lot of houses out there, but it had some of its own sleepy charm.

In Minot, ND we were held up when another train was being serviced at the train depot. The servicing took awhile, and the conductor repeatedly announce we would soon be on our way. Kelly was optimistic, but I was doubtful. I said to my wife, "I think the announcements were just a means of keeping up the morale of the passengers." I suspected we would be waiting for a long time. It's interesting how maintaining the temperament is kind of a communal thing. We have to communicate positivity to a whole body of people to keep spirits in a positive position. Conversely, if you get just a few amongst a group excited and rowdy, dissent spills out into the whole community. When you are in direct contact with a large group of people, as is on a train, communal attitudes become all the more important. This is how mutiny starts: one person gets angry, then the rest follow suite. Attitudes are contagious, and trains are never on time. Hopefully no one there had to be punctual. Hopefully no one was about to lose their temper over the situation. All it would take is one person losing their cool to turn the whole community hostile.

Amtrak is mostly old equipment, in the realm of 30-50 years. Upgrades rely on government subsidies. The money rarely comes in to upgrade train travel. Workers usually live at one end or the other of a particular line. Compensation for workers is generally good, but the company was under-staffed at the time due to the pandemic. As a result, work hours and workloads have been increased. There were also equipment shortages due to no funding to replace equipment that is now no longer functional.

Lack of available equipment results in more limited services; tougher to keep passengers happy. The rail system has one thing going for it: accessibility. The beginning of the National Parks System coincided with the start of the national railroad construction. This simplified logistics of accessing parks by train because they were both developed in close proximity to each other; a dynamic network. It seemed to be to the benefit of Kelly and me.

As we pulled out of Minot, ND at 10:15 AM, tall bluffs accented the topography; arid grasses and wild sunflowers. Even the patches of soil seen looked different, silty, yellow-grey aridisols, characteristic of an arid climate. We trolleyed along a tall bridge for a few hundred yards, and continued through the high plains. Topography alternated between flat and hilly for the next few hours. There were fewer wetlands as we continued out, apparently from steeper slopes producing better drainage. Parts of the land were so flat that if you relaxed your eyes, you could almost see the curvature of the Earth. I finally understood what 10 miles of visibility meant. All the expanse made me regularly consider what fasting would be like in such a place. I wondered what it would be like to be a Plains Indian fasting on those lands on a vision quest. I have done a 3-day fast in the eastern mixed-forest during winter archery season before, and felt mystical power in that. The Plains Indians practiced fasting as a means of vision quest. I feel one would lose themselves to a greater mystical force in such a vast expanse of space. The mind would wander, and the imagination would roam, but how far out would the mind reach without any features on the landscape to provide a sense of relativity?

We passed into the oil fields of North Dakota. They say when times are good the pumps and wells are turning. On that day, about half were turning, and half were not. In the vastness of North Dakota, I began to feel a sense of detachment from humanity and political agendas. That, I was in search of. I was looking for an escape from troubled times. Yes, the trip was about taking an opportunity to adventure while Kelly and I could, but this adventure had greater possibilities than casually viewing national parks. The landscape was telling a story. We brushed the edge of the Missouri River as we crossed from North Dakota into Montana, and the landscape bolstered breathtaking bluffs and escarpments. I see what people mean when they call Montana "Big Sky Country." My perspective took a strange hit as I contemplated the population of the place. Population densities appeared low in MT and ND. Representation in government is often population based. With such low population densities, it made me appreciate that we have both a House of Representatives and a Senate in the federal legislature. U.S. citizens have a bit of luck that exactly 2 senators represent every state in that half of congress. How else would voice be heard? How would we voice our needs and preferences? How would we keep every region of this country strong?

As we got past the town of Glasgow, MT, groves of cottonwoods and oxbow lakes dotted the landscape. Subtle changes in elevation allowed better drainage, and streams to meander and evolve, relocating the stream channel through the course of its evolution. Just before Malta, MT we passed a natural hot springs on the high plains that exhibited steam and a white-sulfur crust. The landscape was foreign and desolate. It was interesting, but not exactly inviting. It looked like this place would produce some very rugged people capable of combating extremes in temperature, privation, and many forms of discomfort. Hot dry land with sage brush and cottonwoods. No sympathy for the devil. This part of the country is supposed to be a hot spot for archeologists looking for dinosaur fossils, and understandably so. The climate can preserve fossil remains extremely well due to how dry everything is. And being so centrally located on a large continent, the collection of specimens would appear to be rather dense. We had a ways to go, another 4 hours on the train or so, but we were slowly closing in on our destination and feasting on the sights just on the other side of our window.

CHAPTER 2

Into the Rockies

The Rocky Mountains are big. They are tall. They are broad. Does that catalyze harmony? Can that defuse fascism and tyranny? I don't know, but they definitely require a man to develop some backbone. Maybe they even make you a little more accountable for your actions and attitude. There is a sense of peace in these mountains that inspires tranquility. That might be a good place to begin. Synchronizing wavelengths, peace and harmony, that takes time to connect with the world around you. Furthermore, it seem the Rocky Mountains have their own way of balancing light and dark energy through the workings of God's hands. In all their ruggedness, the Rockies pull a greater concentration of truth. It's apparent in the dark hollows and towering peaks that humans and the individual are not the end all to be all. It is apparent that there is more to life than what we see in this world.

When we first came into the mountain range on the train, I thought the answer to these questions would appear like magic. They didn't. If answers came, they would be on God's time, the mountain's time. Not my pissy little impulsiveness to know everything at a moment's notice. When night began to fall, and the moon loomed over the dark wild mountains, there I felt an astrological closeness; a relationship between heavenly and earthly bodies. I felt hints of supernatural forces ebbing transcendence. I was coming into a place where Kelly and I would adventure and discover. I would learn things that all other properties of life would stand relative to. I definitely felt small from down in the valley, looking up at the mountain peaks thousands of feet high. It was only just beginning, but I was feeling a sense of the Spirit that lived in these mountains. They appeared so large and rugged that any attempts at greed would only lead to exhaustion. Chasing the carrot over such rough terrain would surely wear you out quicker than you would expect. Lies had no sustenance there. Truth thrived. It flaunted itself. It was handsome and self-reliant. It was the embodiment of radiant beauty that flexed all of its muscles in the dark evening twilight. All that could be gained there was only done so with an honest impression of the self, and an honest impression of where you were in the world.

This rugged landscape inspired exploration, alluring the adventurer into the unknown to discover universal truths. Reflecting on history, something seemed unfair and imbalanced. Why did Europeans sail to America and run out Native Americans? That wasn't their objective, but because of drastic differences, that's what ended up happening. The settlers wanted to stake claim to something that was not theirs, something that could not actually belong to anyone. It was merely a piece of creation that could lead to a closer relationship with the Creator and a fulfilling life here on Earth. Ownership had no honest means of being established, and competition was destroying a heritage of harmony. Fundamentally, the settlers were escaping the Roman Catholic Church. They were seeking religious freedom. They were trying to remove themselves from a church that was ruined by the influx of the government's ideology. Their pursuit was to worship and commune with the spirit in an environment of purity. If anything was to be gained it was to the value of the soul. Could such an industrious culture find harmony in such a natural land? We would hope, but what different people chose to sacrifice to enrich life and soul appeared absolutely incompatible. One people chose to sacrifice urban development. The other people chose to sacrifice harmony on a greater scope. Both pursued passions and liberty, maybe each to their own kind. One preference butted against the next, supposedly. Maybe they all valued the people they lived and associated with, but how far do our associations extend? Beheading people who refused to accept Jesus was not the commission Jesus gave when he told his disciples "Go out, and tell the world about me." Pilgrims were only fleeing tyranny. They did not want to be told what the right way to do things was, but they still had a reverence for the one who made heaven and earth.

As pilgrims set sail to embrace such an ideology, villains would ride on their coat tails and destroy beautiful things in the name of the ego. Conquest came down from royal explorers like Christopher Columbus. What was done in the name of Christ was a cover for what was being done in the name of gold. Conquest and pilgrimage are different. Conquest was set out in the search of resources, not religious freedom. Today we face similar challenges where justice and efficiency appear to be competing objectives. Value of the soul appears to oppose consumer culture and the production of goods where intrinsic value of the natural world is being ignored. They must compete with the demands of convenience and luxury. Nature is the judge who is objective and impartial. That impartial element is the focus in defusing tyranny. Bias judges will favor their own desires and judge accordingly. Objectivity and disinterestedness about decision-making removes passions from defining rules that subjects of the government must live and conduct their behavior by. Spending time with nature will catalyze growth in the soul. We will understand sacrifice and accountability. It all reminds us that there is more to life than what we see in this world. If it were not for European explorers in the 1500 & 1600's, would the Native North American culture survived the industrial revolution? I guess we will never know. If the only objective was religious freedom, the Spirit would have found harmony, harmony between two peoples meeting for the first time; harmony between settlers and the landscape. Still, indigenous tribes all over the world were oppressed and taken advantage of by settlers of every colony throughout all of time.

Newcomer and citizen rarely ever lived in harmony. They did not reflect on the Spirit between the two, how they are different, and how to be pulled toward each other across common ground. Sometimes they did, and those rare relationships were beautiful.

The world over has been subject to the brokenness of the human race. None is more righteous than the other by heritage alone. Differences should be embraced as part of the relationship between people. Unfortunately, colonists did not reflect on the things they already had that could make them happy, like a smile, a handshake, and a good meal. It was the territory rightly occupied by the Natives that was of interest, and greed seemed to provide an ugly impulse to take advantage of kind-hearted people. Religious freedom that brewed into greed and envy does not excuse the conquest of Native peoples. The greed to take land from people burned hot in the souls of some settlers. It was as though they could not find any greater purpose for their lives than conquest.

Righteousness calls us to see beyond ourselves and make sacrifices for the greater good, but what is the greater good? Let us look to universal truths, like the fact that we all matter in God's eyes. I don't know if *each* individual settler was greedy or thirsted for power and domination. Most primarily wanted to worship their God in peace, a God that provided an abundance to those who loved in the Spirit of Christ. They just did not have enough altruism to see beyond their own culture. They couldn't see beyond themselves. The world they lived in had their way with those people. Competition led to the emaciation of Native dominance, and industrial development of their land. Is that supposed to make me feel guilty for being a white male born in the U.S. in the 1980's? I hope not. Still, I feel a sense of discomfort around people of another ethnicity upon initial contact. Not because of them, but because of the way I see myself. It's a discomfort that stems from my expectations of my own behavior. An expectation to behave in a way that is not uncomfortable, disrespectful, or offensive. We must respect everyone, especially when we are in their home. If their home is beautiful and well kept, should we be more inspired to honor and respect? In the Rocky Mountains there is so much beauty and wonder, universal truth appears less territorial and competitive, and more in tune with the soul of a person and the natural landscape they are in, a landscape that can either inspire or punish.

We unboarded the train in Whitefish, Montana around 10:00 PM Tuesday August 2, 2022 and walked close to a mile with packs on backs and totes in hand to our hotel on the edge of town. The walk was about 20 minutes and felt grueling, not knowing where we were going in the dark, nor how far away it was. We hurried along and eventually got to our destination. It was a smallish four-star hotel, clean and stylish. We got our key and went to the room. Kelly and I both showered, then we made love as we crawled into bed around 11:45 PM. Once clean and resting, I reflected on what had passed up until this point. I wasn't clearly understanding what I was trying to decipher. I guess the bigger picture would be enjoying what we had come to experience. I didn't need to solve problems, but it seemed like an incredible opportunity reflect on what was bothering me, and hopefully discover some insight to truth, peace, and harmony. Awesome beauty would surely abound.

CHAPTER 3

First Full Day on the Ground

Kelly and I woke at 7:45 August 3, 2022 in Whitefish, MT, the day we were supposed to get the rental car we would travel in until August 16, 2022. We headed to the streets for breakfast and coffee after doing a little housekeeping. The air smelled a little different and felt warm. The sun was shining down on the town of Whitefish, quite a charming mountain town in the Northern Rockies. The town was quaint and well-kept. A good coffee shop had to be around there somewhere. The town just had that kind of feel. Walking down the streets and past storefronts, we sought out Montana Coffee Traders. It was spacious and well kept. The interior design of the place reflected the mountain town. There, Kelly and I ordered a red-eye, a vanilla latte, BLT's, and a pound of beans to make coffee in our percolator on the days we would camp. The food was delicious, and the coffee was high quality. The coffee shop and all the stores were clean and up to date, yet exhibited a rustic face. Things were just starting out, but they were already exhilarating. The weather and landscape couldn't have been more beautiful. Feeling fat and happy we walked the town that gorgeous August morning. It was the perfect starting point for what would come over the next two and a half weeks. I was reeling in our dimension of time and space. I felt like I could fly from the immediate diet and landscape. The blood was pumping, and the natural stimulation sent thoughts and sensations through my being that were liberating, and it was exactly the stuff I had in mind when we started planning this trip.

All the anticipation came to a head as the future became the present. We were living the dream. By 9:45 AM we were heading back to the hotel to receive our car and made a quick detour to explore a riverwalk on the edge of town. We got the car, our adventure-mobile, a 2021 blue Hyundai Tucson. After loading up the car with our gear we ran to a store for all the supplies for the trip: folding chairs, bug spray, garbage bags, bear spray, toiletries. We didn't pack much in the way of soap and shampoo. We figured we could buy that stuff after we got the car to cut down pack space and carrying weight while on the train. The shopping went smoothly, although Kelly and I compromised with each other on a thing or two. We had a hard time finding sunscreen, and the lady at Walgreens told us the population of Whitefish triples in the summer months due to tourism, so, according to her, it should have been no surprise that we were having trouble finding the stuff anywhere.

Tourism felt like it wears on the locals of Whitefish who find employment in the retail and hospitality industries. They, at least some of them, wear a bristly exterior, but still seem to appreciate generosity and thoughtfulness. Being a *local* in a tourist town holds a much different perspective than a *tourist* in a tourist town. Travelers hustling to get resources and information can be exhausting for the ones who provide those services day in and day out. I was a raft guide in a river town for a season, so I know the feel and have heard the opinions of the locals from behind closed doors. A place of holiday for one and a place of burden for another create contrasting perspectives for people sharing the same location. We should all be patient and grateful for the sacrifices anyone makes to help us along.

After lunch in a saloon in Whitefish we headed to our chalet, Silver Wolf Log Chalets, just outside the west gate of Glacier National Park. It was about a 40-minute drive. We rode through the Flathead River Valley, and I commented to Kelly how truly awesome it would be to be a Native American living in the valley 1,000 years ago before any influence of white people. The mountainsides towered overhead with enormous cliffs jutting out of the face of the mountain. The lush green valley spread wide from the river's edge, just up to the mountains overhead. We continued down U.S. route 2 to our chalet. Silver Wolf Log Chalets were quaint, cozy, and rustic; romantic in a minimalist and natural sort of way. Andrew at the front desk let us into the place. He was a very welcoming middle-aged man giving us the skinny of the locality. From him, we gathered that: weed is acceptable in most situations, summer highs are in the area of 100 degrees F, winter lows are around 0 degrees F, not a lot of snow in the winter, and locals by large have a self-sustaining, pull yourself up by own bootstraps, mentality. Lots of outdoor guides and horse packers regulared West Glacier, MT... roughnecks.

After seeking out our accommodations and dropping our gear, we headed into Glacier National Park around 3:30 PM. We were near the west gate to the park near the Lake McDonald area. Kelly had a map and chose for us a hike that wasn't *too* remote. It took a quick minute to get our bearings once in the park, but after a little scrambling we found the trail head for the Rocky Point overlook trail. The road network within Glacier National Park was sprawling, over 1,583 square miles of land. A few major roads connected one end from another, with branches shooting off into different regions of GNP. Rocky Point was one of the off-shoots of Going to the Sun Road near the western entrance. The overlook was a mile into the trail, and part of a larger trail loop. By this point I was getting familiar with the vegetation, but the topography continued to leave a fresh impression on me. Most slopes weren't much steeper than in the Appalachians and Laurel Highlands, but mountain was butted against water with many high peaks, and more cliff faces. I was in my glory as we made that first hike. When we came to Rocky Point upon Lake McDonald, I lost myself. I took the conscious effort to release anything that might have been in my mind and tried to immerse myself in the ethos of the place. The coniferous forest and rocky soil were sending me into a sun-brazen state of mind despite only hiking for an hour or two that first day. In total we spent about two and half hours on the trail and along Lake McDonald that first afternoon, but it was the beginning of something that would be absolutely incredible.

The first night in town, we ate dinner at a roadhouse called The Packer's Roost. We had burgers and drank craft brew brown ale, Moose Drool. After dinner, we went back to the chalet. I was taken by the romanticism of our rustic accommodations. A nice little hideaway. Kelly got showered and I sat on the front porch. It was around dark, just a little before 10:00 PM. I thought about daylight and latitude, contemplating the fact that most of the world lives between 23 degrees and 66 degrees north or south latitude. This places most of the world in a moderate setting when it comes to the extremes of daylight. Above the arctic circle (or below the Antarctic if you so wish) the sun never sets on the summer solstice, and daylight extends well into nighttime hours due to the curvature of Earth's sphere. The further you get away from the equator, the longer the days are in the summer, and the shorter they are in the winter. Length of day can play tricks on the way the mind relates to the landscape. In summer, you feel like you have endless energy. Evening twilight at 10:00 PM creates an illusion that despite being late, there is still plenty of opportunity for the day to provide. Also rising around 5:00 AM and the sky already being light energizes the mind as you wake early from sleep and get ready for the day.

In my moments contemplating on the porch that night, a valley breeze blew upward from downslope as the air on top the mountain cooled earlier and rushed down pushing warm air up from the valley below. It was an invigorating feeling. I have not been in such large mountains to experience something like this before. The trees and vegetation swayed in the evening twilight breeze, and I could feel myself shaking off the bounds of society. Being in such a vast, rugged, and remote space sent chills down my spine. The night air was enchanting, and the sky held promise. There were quite a lot of stars in the sky; a night to remember.

CHAPTER 4

Going to the Sun Road

When in Glacier National Park, you will say "Oh wow!" So much so, that Kelly and I renamed the park "Oh Wow!" Going to the Sun Road is 49.7 miles that connects the east side of the park to the west side of the park, crossing Logan Pass and the continental divide along the way. There are spectacular views all along, and you can only respond with, "Oh wow!" We entered Going to the Sun Road from the west entrance on the morning of August 4, 2022 around 7:30 AM. The ranger at the entrance was very charismatic as were all the rangers we came in contact with. I feel all the rangers in the national park system have to pass a friendliness certification as a pre-requisite for employment. They are all nice and happy. There is so much to do in this park. People who love hiking, photography, camping, cycling, horseback riding, kayaking, and just being in nature have spectacular opportunities in Glacier National Park. Enter and experience.

We started up Going to the Sun Road along the edge of Lake McDonald, a long, skinny, glacial lake about 5-10 miles long. Looking up the valley from the mouth, this and every other lake in the park creates a unique perspective. You have an aspect from the baseline elevation of surface water. Valley walls rise up all around you. And high above, far in the distance, tower majestic glacial peaks thousands of feet over head. At the headwaters of Lake McDonald is Upper McDonald Creek. We stopped at Sacred Dancing Cascade around 8:00 AM on Upper McDonald Creek. The sight from the road caught our interest, and we stopped for a picture and a closer look. The cascade is a class IV whitewater cascade with a class III runout at the bottom. The steep rushing water was mesmerizing as white spray splashed and the river collided with the rocks. Seeing the drop made me want to fire up something in my kayak. I was seeing a lot of ocean kayaks on the roofs of cars for paddling the glacial lakes in the park. The lakes are too rough to accommodate recreational kayaks. Something a little more aggressive and skillful would be required to set out on these waters. Even the lakes looked turbulent from the shores.

2–3-foot waves cut across the surface making it challenging water to paddle. So many people are drawn to the park for honest, innocent, and pure reasons, like hiking and kayaking. Maybe it's the best method in this country to escape the institutions of society: sports, entertainment, media, politics, money. With release from the hostility found in those institutions of society, into a natural landscape of innocent pleasure, we begin to breathe on a more harmonious wavelength. In the beginning, one is ebbing and flowing ever so subtly, but after a while, one notices the changes in their soul. The park offers something spiritual, but the mountain doesn't give up her secrets at a moment's notice. Quality time in communion is necessary.

Incredible wonder. It makes you feel small, sounds cliché, I know, but you must experience it to understand it. Hopefully the words on this page are capable of inspiring something close to what the mountains were making Kelly and me feel inside. Wonder is a stance of appreciation to the God who made it all, through all of His laws of nature, and the mechanics of his handiwork. With a heart posture of gratitude, and a humble relationship of feeling less than something else, we begin to see beyond ourselves. Appreciating what has been done, things no human nor all of humanity could do, in the greatness of creation positions us with a more honest perspective where universal truths are more evident. I only *know* two things: 1) water runs downhill, and 2) summer is warmer than winter. God is the great physicist. All laws of nature bow to his will; momentum, gravity, convection, conduction, etc. His character is embodied in creation, and we can begin to observe this in the patterns we see in nature. With a perspective beholding His Spirit as the conjoined forces of energy and consciousness, we get a clearer picture of who the Creator is. He forces the architecture of the landscape and instills harmony between us and it. Sometimes God speaks, and leads you places. You might not understand why at first, but you end up finding incredible and glorious things. The amazement results in a mental condition I would like to call "Post Wonder Cognitive Disorder." It transcends all pre-conceived notions of who you thought God was, and what exactly He is capable of. You are placed into a new frame of mind where everything in life is relative to this new maximum of inspiration and amazement.

As we drove up the west face of Going to the Sun Road, Chinook Winds were strong. We were gaining elevation towards Logan Pass seeing incredible views. The glaciated mountain peaks were breathtaking, carved angular sedimentary rocks. God made all of this for us, for our wonder and amazement, to feel connected, to feel beautiful and loved, and also to remind us of who we are. In these places we can reflect on the environment around us, ourselves, and the harmony that exists between the two. It was there to inspire us. To enlighten us. To fill us with joy, wonder, and reverence. It was a little nerve-racking driving up Going to the Sun Road, as the road is nothing more than a ledge cut into the face of a mountain. That was not unique to the park as many roads in northwest Montana are cut along a ledge, but Going to the Sun Road is a sheer cliff that plummets down thousands of feet to the valley floor. Going to the Sun Road gets even sketchier as you gain elevation. It was not as rough as some of the shuttle roads I have driven for whitewater kayaking in Pennsylvania and West Virginia, but clinging to the ledge had me on edge. I was only going 25 mph or less at all times. That first day was tense on Going to the Sun Road. It would have been nice to let my guard down and take in the sights.

All the rock I saw that day was sedimentary in nature: sandstone, limestone, shale. Differing degrees of heat and pressure left some of the bedrock argillic. It was borderline metamorphic geology in different parts of the park. Some bedrock appeared harder, more tightly bound, polished, and tabular in appearance. Glacier was a geologist's dream. Great mountain peaks rising all around the 1,500 square mile park, plenty of opportunity to observe and study. Amongst the beauty and remoteness of it all, there was a reverence. One just has to give it time to let it come over them. On Logan Pass, the air had a serious mountain smell to it. Dust, sand, and gravel sailed in the wind at that high elevation. Impressive. It kept me on guard as it pelted the car while driving the road. The geology was explicit in its expression, spelling out the environments which formed it for anyone who had deeper understanding of what they were looking at. Throughout the mountain range there are engaging features for the naturalist: wildlife, vegetation, forest, water, rocks. Many levels for observation, reflection, and connection... Three elements integral in the study of nature.

Vastness is something hard to grasp until you are in it. At the top of Going to the Sun Road, we were in the vastness. It took our breath away, and we transcended beyond everything we thought we knew. There was a reverence that filled us, serenity, and feeling very small in relation to it. The landscape was different beyond Logan Pass, starting down the east face of the mountain to St. Mary Lake; redbeds, dead conifers, open understory. Even down to St. Mary Lake the wind was strong and consistent. The car said 73F, but with the windchill, the air felt cooler than 60F. As we continued to descend, life came back to the conifers. The pines were distributed spaciously, and grassland filled the gaps between the trees. I've never seen such a large area of land so wild and untamed. It's easy to see where some of the Native American mysticism comes from, contemplating the Spirit in such a place. Feeling small I was inspired by awe and wonder, partially unable to conceive what forces could create such a landscape. Time, matter, space, it was all involved. Beauty was at the face of both the Creator and the Creation. An element of privation affected it all, as one considered it through the mind's eye and let the essence of the landscape flood your soul. The ethos of both its creation and existence could not have been cognized without experiencing it. And with the experience, I now had a relationship with something so great, and so integral to being American.

At 2:00 PM I saw the biggest mountains I've ever seen in my life. It was ridgelines dissected by glaciation forming numerous peaks. The peaks were separated by saddles and valleys in wide breath. Vegetation of mostly grasses and flowers covered the gentler slopes. Bare bedrock was present on the steeper areas and areas above the treeline due to atmosphere or a lack of soil. Smatterings of coniferous forest could be seen at the foothills and transitions. The vastness of it all was incredibly impressive and completely breathtaking. We took lots of pictures and stood in awe at the foot of the mountain. We were observing geology. Geology is spectacular and raises curiosity, but the hardest part to comprehend is the amount of time it takes to bring mountain formations into existence, and eventually weather them away to modest hills. Stratigraphy, characterizing layers of different rock, has a way to amaze a rock-nerd. It tells a story of time, energy, and composition. Layers and colors are obvious, but when you start analyzing them, they tell you something much deeper about the long-ago world in which they were formed.

Chinook Winds kept up at 25-35 mph through the afternoon. Dark clouds loomed overhead, and it started spitting rain as we stood above Swiftcurrent Lake in the northeast corner of the park taking pictures. On our way out of the Swiftcurrent Lake area, we saw a mama grizzly and two cubs walking down a steep talus slope about 300 yards away as high winds and rain pushed through. Not long before, in the same area, a couple behind us said they saw a black bear come down off the hill and cross the road nearby. It might have had something to do with impending squalls, bears moving from higher elevations to lower elevations to seek shelter from the storm. Animals are more in tune with pressure gradients and changes in weather. They are forced to take cover wherever the landscape might provide it. The bears were definitely on the move, moving toward thick brush, rock ledges and caves and hollows.

We did the 8-mile distance between Babb and St. Mary 6 times that day waiting for parking to clear out at the Swiftcurrent trailhead. One of the many challenges in experiencing the park is traffic and access. The volume of visitors is much greater than available parking. People come early and spend all day on the trail. When they leave, it's one by one, not many at a time. So, available parking fills up just as quick. Still, I don't think any park visitor wants to see more land cleared for the sake of parking. One of the most impressive things about the park is despite its mostly untamed landscape, there are accessible features amongst the rugged terrain. The challenge is more so from the volume of people cramming into limited space. The accessibility in places away from the front country was developed just enough to draw hikers in, give them a place to roam, and maintain a low impact. It speaks something about how well-planned developing the park was. Bushwhacking the trails and trailheads had to take an intimate understanding of landscape and topography with extremely good mapping before the start. Breathtaking hikes appeared to be seamlessly in place. Getting places only took motivation. Parking was available for early risers. All trails left us in awe and wonder. Amidst it all there is a matter of conservation that has to be kept to the natural ruggedness of the park while setting up enough infrastructure to accommodate the crowds which the landscape was sure to attract. Balance needed to be met, and they did a good job achieving that, at least for the ambitious and adventurous types. All the natural beauty was just absolutely incredible. Experiencing a place like Glacier should be enough to appreciate all God has given us. It should be enough for us to thirst for the things of Heaven, things believed in yet unseen, but having the palate wet just enough by the sheer beauty that places such as this might incur. With such desires, it should also be natural for us to fear being deprived of wonderful things such as this in the afterlife, should any of us receive eternal damnation.

CHAPTER 5

Two Medicine and the Aster Park Trail

Spirit imparts consciousness. Consciousness imparts personality, and personality imparts conduct. Therefore, Spirit imparts conduct. Spirit effectually is composed of consciousness and energy. Heat, light, kinetic energy, etc. and the character and habit of those things. The character of conscious spirit can be observed in patterns we see in nature, and the cycles we see in nature. When we allow an element of naturalness to permeate into our being, our conduct will follow that path of naturalness. It is important to follow the patterns of nature, not the patterns of society. Believing in the supernatural and patterning after nature will lead to appreciation for it all. That is a good beginning point in developing a relationship with Holy Spirit and imparting good conduct. Would that allow us to exist on a more harmonious level, living by the Spirit? Would that be existing on more harmonious wavelengths? Would that allow for more balance of light and dark in the world? I would hope so. Believing in the supernatural and patterning after nature could bring more balance to our lives. The world would benefit from people interacting with ecotourism and outdoor adventure. That would separate us from corrupt institutions of society.

In community and fellowship we show compassion and celebrate the universal truths that nature teaches us. We should not follow the evil that exists in this world. It is primarily personality that drives tyranny and oppression; personality derived from the spirit within, producing a conduct of tyranny. The ultimate force of spirit has the power to override bad conduct and sour personality. It is a force of goodness flowing through us. The Holy Spirit is what Christ descended to Earth to bring us, but only after he was crucified then resurrected to glory. Spirit has to be believed in and accepted. It has to be brought into our lives. Then conditions our hearts and minds through the activities and environments we immerse ourselves in. Some people should be forced to engage in outdoor adventure to feel the reverence for its power, power to enlighten us and humble us. Nature shows no favorites. We all exist under a common natural law, and some need to be reminded by nature that some laws can never be broken, no matter what. The natural landscape is often a reflection of the human spirit. The mountains are rugged. We are made in the image of God's strength. The mountains are beautiful and serene. We have been made in the image of God's love. It says these things in the Bible. All things work according to God's will; our limits, our abilities, the laws of nature. It is all done by the energy and consciousness of His Spirit.

On Friday August 5, 2022, Kelly and I hiked the Aster Park Trail in the Two Medicine area of Glacier National Park. On the map Kelly and I scoped out this trail that had a waterfall and a scenic overlook. We had no expectations of what the natural landscape would do inside of us. We were acclimating to the Northern Rockies. The topography and vegetation were imparting their consciousness upon us. Upon embarking, the peace derived from the elevation and the forest saturated my soul. The only bad thing was how talkative we had to be to alert grizzlies of our presence, and not surprise them should we come across one. As I talked to Kelly, I was trying to rationalize the way the environment was making me feel inside. The words felt superfluous to the natural wonder before me. We use words like "wonderful," "awesome," and "beautiful," but are often used so loosely that they are almost spoken in vain. They lose effectiveness even when in situations as transcendental as being in Glacier National Park.

From Upper Two Medicine Lake, we started down the Aster Park trail. Sinopah Mtn. towered at the head of the glacial U-shaped valley with Mt. Rockwell just to the southwest about ½ a mile ahead. The trail rolled across gently undulating topography with grasses, flowers, and fir trees filling the ecosystem. The green and bright forest was welcoming and felt comfortable, even a little mystical in morning light. There was sweetness in the air and peace in our hearts. It was serene and captivating. The way the light filtered through the lush green forest warmed the soul in some western American fashion. Everything I learned up to this point was being compiled in my mind as I was making observations and discoveries of my own. The rock-nerd in me was being activated. There were sedimentary rocks that almost appeared metamorphic upon closer inspection. I eyed small red quartzite cobbles as Kelly curiously questioned me about the geology. The sun was bright that morning as it illuminated the beautiful forest. We crossed Aster Creek and the waters were incredibly clear. They sparkled with priceless transparency. Red, grey, and tan cobbles and pebbles could be seen in the creek bed beneath its cool, clean waters. Two golden-mantled ground-squirrels were wrestling and playing along the trail. We saw many ground squirrels that day, and in places, the trees felt like a community the way they were spread out. The morning was incredible; more than I could put to words. Freedom was flowing, and there was no way of avoiding it. We were communing, immersing ourselves in the natural wonder. The beauty of the place was captivating, and the vastness was breathtaking, a great expanse to roam with terrain so rugged that it oozed strength from the mountains and their creator into our human spirits. I cannot fully capture the spirit of the place in writing. It was too wild.

Walking through the Eden of Glacier National Park, there is clarity. The weather was like September in the Appalachians; hot days, cool mornings, sunny skies and dry air. The atmosphere generated a more untamed feeling. The clarity increased as we gained elevation. The trail we were on was not an easy stroll the whole way. After Aster Falls, the trail began to climb the mountain and switched back and forth across the hillside as we gained 600 feet in elevation. On that clear August morning, the feeling of the forest was warm and fuzzy, and as we continued, it became something more, approaching ethereal. Standing in the creek at the bottom of Aster Falls, I felt in place. I felt like God specifically put me in that spot in that exact moment in time for a purpose. Mountains towered overhead. Trees and plants engulfed us. The water and sunshine shimmered. Tranquility filled our hearts. As soon as we stepped into the shadowy forest about 80 vertical feet above the lake, the air got noticeably cooler. Seeing the treeline end and the mountains continue up put things in perspective. The elevation of the glacial peaks was impressive. They inspired awe, wonder, and pursuit. The spirit of the place was spelled out explicitly before us.

At one point, amongst the atmosphere and landscape, the only emotion I could describe was pure joy. It is said joy, true joy, only comes from the presence of the Lord, not our circumstances. That morning I felt more in the presence of the Lord than in circumstance of time and space. The energy and consciousness of Two Medicine could be sensed and traced back to a unified and singular source, God, and presented in a unique and specialized product of supernatural Spirit, Glacier National Park. It was impressed upon our souls as we experienced it. The experience brought us closer to God and gave us a clearer vision of a finite and specialized facet of the Holy Spirit. God, Jesus Christ, and the Holy Spirit are what true Christians adhere to.

It seems a little funny reflecting on Jesus while hiking in the high country, but Jesus came to the world for a few reasons: 1) Calm the evil that the devil was brewing up in this world up to the first century A.D. and correct the course of social evolution. 2) Condition the culture to love each other in truth, laying aside the law and dogma of the Jewish religion, to tell us God loves us, and we should love each other; to make the unclean clean 3) Forgive us of our sins by dying on the cross, and ascending to heaven on the third day. 4) To share the Holy Spirit with all who believe in Him after he rose to glory. 5) Giving God a human face to identify with. Christ Jesus rose from the grave to fill us with the same spirit that forged all creation, to give us joy in this life, and create a path to heaven for all who believe in in him in word and deed. What would heaven look like? I think that is fair to contemplate, maybe even speculate upon, but little if anything should be assumed about Heaven. It might be a place at least as glorious as Glacier National Park. That would be fine with me and Kelly. Furthermore, it says no one will enter heaven unless they enter with the innocence and eyes of a child. Humble yourselves before the Lord.

At the top of Aster Park Trail, Kelly and I sat on a shelf overlooking Upper Two Medicine Lake from 600 feet above. On the opposite side of the lake was Rising Wolf Mtn. 9,513 feet above sea level. The wind from the day before had died down. The sun was shining. The birds were singing in sparse notes. We were in the high country seeing forever. I never felt so small. I felt at one with the Earth. The morning coolness gave way to 80F temps midday. We were still on the trail around noon. Things definitely got hotter and brighter. It was evident that we were high up in the mountains in an arid climate. Thin air and brilliant blue sky. It was a beautiful August Montana afternoon. Time and space came together to compose a phenomenon that was unique and connected us to the moment. Sunlight was less intense in the morning on our way in.

On our way out, we saw a moose eating in a swamp along a meadow down in the glacial valley. The animal was very large yet a little over 100 yards away. The swamp water met the edge of the surrounding vegetation, and the animal had its own pocket to eat and wallow in the brilliant day with calf standing nearby at the water's edge. The climate felt unique to that place, but so did the vegetation and geology, too. I couldn't imagine anyone wanting to take away or destroy something so beautiful. We can only pray the ego would never drive a person to do such things. It's great that our government had enough mind to preserve and protect lands such as our national parks and national forests.

In national forests, you can hunt, but you can't in national parks. Hunting is a practice of pursuit and harvest. It requires harmonizing with the wavelengths of your surroundings to close in on game. You move at the rhythm of the forest. It sounds barbaric to some, but nothing, absolutely nothing, comes without sacrifice. The honesty of pursuit leaves more appreciation towards the things being sacrificed, and I don't think it's somehow holier to spill the blood onto someone else's hands. Furthermore, in taking the life of an animal to put food on the table you see life being sacrificed and appreciate the life that has been given to you for your own benefit. In this way, most hunters become sensitive to the differences between life and death. Hunting teaches a person a lot, and all the first civilizations of the world understood these teachings. Now these traditions are being lost to time because the means by which society operates is signaling these values as hateful and barbaric. What is barbaric is being ignorant of what it takes to put food on the table. Original cultures were developed upon these values and had sound character because of it, and by its conditioning. These traditions have been carried through time, but will they always be around to teach us the important lessons of life?

We got off the trail around 1:00 PM and had lunch at the Whistle Stop just outside the park in East Glacier. It was casual dining with an outdoor deck and picnic tables. Our waitress was Native American. Kelly and I both got bison burgers and huckleberry pie. I got a coffee as well. We returned to Two Medicine after lunch and took a short hike later in the day. The trail was the Running Eagle trail at the base of Upper Two Medicine Lake. The trail was 0.3 miles one way. It was mostly flat and wheelchair accessible. A stream about 50 feet wide poured out of the base of the lake and flowed along the trail. It was rocky with sandstone cobble and aridisols on the banks. We basked in the sun letting the afterglow of the morning hike carry us through and we shifted into autopilot as mind and body had been fatigued by the day. We hung out until about 4:00 PM, then took U.S. Route 2 back to our chalet on the other side of the park. For two hours, the road wound around the mountains giving way to spectacular views of the northwest Montana countryside. We saw a black bear along the way and rode maybe 10 miles behind a pilot truck leading us through a construction zone where the length of the road was nothing but dirt and gravel.

Craig Leibfreid

We went to the Packers' Roost for dinner that night and enjoyed the peace and serenity of our chalet after we ate and drank. We were rather joyous as we reflected on the day we spent in the park and digressed to the night, jolly and satisfied.

CHAPTER 6

Hidden Lake and Logan Pass

The power of good communication bridges gaps, connecting us with each other, and allowing for love to flow more freely. Good communication requires us to listen first, be empathetic, and think about what we're going to say before we say it. We must take on the other person's perspective before we can actually give wise advice. Seeing things from their point of view can shed light on regions of truth not seen before. Make it about them at least as much as it is about ourselves. Otherwise, we are pushing our own thoughts and opinions onto another person. We are not living a moment in another person's shoes and providing insightful solutions. You could blame selfishness, but a greater part of the problem is impulse. Sometimes our response is ruled by our emotions. That is not healthy. We impulsively try to validate ourselves by tuning out the other and tuning in the self.

There are tools to control impulses. Meditation is one. It teaches us patience, the ability to let go of thoughts, and helps give us the ability to see beyond ourselves. If we control our impulses and don't distract ourselves through pleasurable indulgences, we are making sacrifices in our character that build self-control and teach us patience. Faith and a relationship with God are other good ways of learning self-control and seeing beyond ourselves. It is a means of making ourselves accountable for the lives we live. It is not something to sit upon boasting while becoming luke-warm in our faith, and complacent. Mature faith can deteriorate by attaching ourselves to expectations of forgiveness. Honesty is the first step towards discipline. To be fair and honest are the first steps toward righteousness.

Saturday morning, we woke at 5:45 and headed for Logan Pass. Logan Pass sits on the continental divide on the Going to the Sun Road. The parking lot at the trailhead is said to fill up by 8:00 AM, which, it was full when we arrived at 8:15. The skies were clear and the air was cool that morning. I had a layer on over my tee shirt when we set out from the chalet. We laced up our boots, and threw our packs in the car. The mountain that morning was some strange combination of peace and excitement. A purity and innocence could be felt as we climbed the slopes in our car, up to the divide. The elevation and the weather sent me into euphoria. I could feel a deep sense of peace, and I think Kelly and I were on the same wavelength. Like I said, when we arrived at the Logan Pass parking lot at 8:15, there were no open spaces. We drove down the east face of the mountain about ¾ of a mile and took the last parking spot in that particular pull-off.

We hiked back the ¾ mile up the road to the trailhead in the cool morning air. The tread under the foot felt good. Trudging up the slopes, we began harmonizing with the environment. Atmosphere and landscape were ebbing in the soul in a summer sunrise high country sort of way. Engaging in physical activity was catalyzing the vibes coming from the mountain. The energy was activated. All there was left to do was synchronize. We were in a place with a vantage point of incredible expanse. We were close to the top of the mountain, and we could see other peaks miles away. About halfway up the mile long trail to the Hidden Lake overlook, I chilled out. I mean I felt *really* chill. That was moments before we saw a mountain goat about 20 yards away at the top of the pass to Hidden Lake, such a mystical creature. As I stood there watching the goat, I could feel the Holy Spirit. It was other-worldly. I could not critique the moment to any conclusion. It was recklessly transcendental. The goat practically looked into my soul, and as he approached, he filled me with a sensation so foreign, yet so divine that I could not turn away or forget. The mountain goat brought the landscape to life. It was engaging, and trying to ignore it or see beyond it would be nothing more than an insult to God. It would be an insult to the chill zone. Not that the "chill zone" is a very finite place, but after 3 ½ days in the park, I finally received the sensation I came for. The ethos of Glacier National Park filled me filled me in a deep, deep sense, and there was nothing left of Craig but an emotion of natural tranquility and a bit of curiosity. It was the power of good communication between hiker and landscape. I was listening to the environment while I walked along to the rhythm of the day.

The slope up to the overlook had lots of red limestone and red shale. The geology continued to impress. The glacial valley was roughly 5 miles wide and who knows how long. It was mostly grassland with clusters of conifers, flowers, and exposed rock. Very open landscape up to Hidden Lake. I fell into a state I truly relished. It was akin to something I didn't know existed, but at the same time was always after. Part of it was being there with my wife. Part of it was the Spirit that God filled me with. Part of it was being immersed in that environment for 3 ½ days. Part of it was walking 2 miles uphill with the sun shining and an extremely vast view. Those four things did not have a difference in opinion. Mostly because they were rooted all in the same thing: the primal source for all creation. And they communicated to and through each other. It was very important to listen to the things they had to say, for, now, I understand myself better, and will love better because I have listened to what those other things desire.

Bearhat Mountain laid immediately on the opposite side of Hidden Lake from where we approached on the trail. Reynolds Mountain was almost 1 mile to the south, to the left of the trail, as we hiked in, and Clements Mountain was immediately to our north, our right, while we were at the overlook, immediately at its foot. We stood at the pass between Reynolds Mtn. and Clements Mtn. looking 675 ft. down at Hidden Lake. The difference in elevation didn't feel quite that big, but probably because of the vastness in a horizontal senses skewing the frame of reference. The lake was a crescent carved into the base of a few contiguous mountains by glaciation at a relatively high elevation. Bear activity is said to be high near the lake in the spring and summer months. We didn't hike down to the lake because the trail was closed that day due to bear activity. From the trail head to the overlook is a 1.3-mile uphill hike. It climbs 550 vertical feet. Along the way, we saw purple daisies growing out of rocks, and a ram bighorn sheep eating below a talus slope. The alpine glacial landscape exhibited horns, cirques, and aretes, hanging valleys, and long U-shaped valleys, sometimes filled with water to make alpine glacial lakes. It all flowed together across the mountain range. Every place on this earth has a unique sight and feel. Glacier National Park was no different, and it felt like a gem. It felt like sanctuary. It has the means of transcendence, dazing you with its logic, pondering its development, function, and future for great lengths of time.

We hiked from 8:30-12:00 that day and got lunch and coffee in St. Mary at the east entrance of the Going to the Sun Road.

On our way back into the park that afternoon, we popped into Sun Point on Lake St. Mary. Sun point was at the base of the mountain where the gradual slope began to get steeper. Lake St. Mary laid at the same crux where the slope transitioned. Steep cliffs sat at its edge, one of which was Sun Point. Lots of barren rock and a little pine and grasses littered the edge of the lake. We spent about an hour hiking and taking in the views on that beautiful, sunny day at Sun Point.

Afterward, we got back in the car and crossed up and over the divide, then down to the foot of the west face to hike the Trail of the Cedars. The ecosystems of the opposing and adjacent watersheds of the park exhibited such great variability. The weather and soil definitely exhibited some variation across the expanse of mountain. Soil depth and the rate of weathering felt minimal. So little water for hydrolysis, and such variation amongst types of topography. Trail of the Cedars was a 1-mile loop over a mostly flat boardwalk. It is almost entirely open mature pine forest with western red cedar, western hemlock, and black cottonwood populating the community. Trail of the Cedars is a smaller portion of the Avalanche Trail area of the park. The area hosts the eastern-most temperate rainforest in the U.S. The temperatures were relatively cool with plenty of shade and Avalanche Creek dissecting the loop. That little area of the park doesn't seem to get more precipitation than the rest of the park. It might, but it seems to exhibit less evapotranspiration. It is also protected from fire by topography and geology, which probably also accounts for the low evapotranspiration rates. Avalanche Creek cuts a streambed through the middle of the trail loop, and lots of cobble line the bed and the banks of the stream. These rocks came from higher up the slope as the bedrock of the mountain weathered and broke apart, allowing the water and gravity to carry them downhill. That little watershed appeared both rugged and soft as the cool shady coniferous forest encapsulated the ragged rock faces and stream bed.

On the boardwalk, I stopped to put notes into my phone when, blind to me, foot traffic picked up in a hurry from both directions. Somebody passing by said something disrespectful to me as I was in their way, and it made me think: when life gets busy, the likelihood for people to get impulsive, disrespectful, and short-tempered increases. We should always be ready for chaos and the ability to deal with it patiently. Not by anxiously stressing over the future, but by *meditatively* holding control over your impulses. We could all do well to set aside a little time every day to disconnect, meditate, and see beyond ourselves. "We should meditate with a miniscule perspective to discover God's light shining within us, and a cosmic perspective to realize the smallness of our existence within the universe" – Ryuho Okawa. Reflection of this should cause us to postulate out and connect us with our surroundings. It aids in communication because it is not I unto you. It is an exchange between you and I, an exchange along harmonious wavelengths. If we connect with our surroundings, finding and sustaining harmony is much easier. The natural world before us feels like a reflection of the human spirit at times. There is restraint, mystery, strength, and resiliency. Things that take place in these natural environments are relatively unknown without setting aside the time to communicate; study and reflect. And like observing natural beauty, we should take time to make observations within ourselves. Furthermore, understanding that both it and us come from a common source connects us all, and ought to allow a coalescing of diversity, creating a beautiful mosaic across the landscape.

CHAPTER 7

Swiftcurrent Pass Trail

The hydrosphere on Earth consists of water vapor, groundwater, ice, snowpack, lakes, oceans, and of rivers and watersheds. They all are all connected networks of moving water. Glacial advance and retreat, flowing rivers, ocean tides, groundwater percolation, all of it. They are all in constant flux. Water and glacial ice sculpt the surface of Earth, and transport nutrients and sediment along Earth's crust. H2O is also one of the greatest insulators of heat energy here on Earth. Looking at a map, the east face of Glacier National Park looks dendritic in its drainage, and the west face of the divide looks trellis in its drainage. It was not completely evident from the front country how the streams sourced the water. The high peaks were above the water table, so it didn't look like groundwater popping out of the land's surface was the water source of the creeks and rivers. Groundwater breaching land's surface is typically how the water is sourced in streams in humid climates, like the Appalachian Mountains. Glacier National Park gets ample snowpack. Many peaks are still covered by snow in early August. Alpine glaciers have been retreating over the past few decades and centuries. It seems there is always snow melting, even through the summer months, that provides the source of surface water in the creeks and rivers of the park. Water channels in Glacier are long, steep, and sometimes vertical. It could be 3,000 ft. in elevation in places from the point where snow melts on a peak until it reaches the river at the bottom of the glacial valley. Along the way, much of the drop could be straight down, allowing water and gravity to reshape the rock formations. The landscape is always changing, but that takes time, time to elapse between cause and effect. Subtle changes through time are how God develops the landscape. He is a patient Creator. As follows we should be patient with each other, just as God is patient with us, patient for us to turn away from bad behavior and any disrespect.

You need at least three full days in the park to get the full effect. That gives you time to disconnect from where you came and reconnect to where you have landed. It takes time and focus to acclimate. The quicker you release yourself from the institutions that held you, the quicker you will harmonize with this amazingly beautiful land you are now in. At some point on day 3 ½ we completely lost who we were and found reformation and restoration in the wilds of Glacier National Park. Day 3 ½ was the day of hiking to Hidden Lake and seeing the mountain goats. At that point, the necrotic husk from decaying spirit withered away. Stacks of responsibility and the institutions of man withered away and something glorious regenerated in its place. I was inching closer to the existence God had in mind for humans when he created the world. Spending quality time in nature reconditioned the mind, body, and spirit to its glorious source of origination. It was a feeling of restoration. It's like becoming dead to sin and being reborn in Jesus. I can't wrap my head around why people would rather go to places like Las Vegas where greed and impulse are paramount and encouraged instead of the beautiful wilds of this natural country. They are compounding compositions of the institutions of man; things far less than what the Holy Spirit can deliver. Sin city is rather vapid and hollow when compared to places like Glacier National Park. We put money, sex, and entertainment before God, and history will prove nothing angers Him more than our sinful idols.

On day 4 ½ we arrived at Many Glacier to hike the Swiftcurrent Pass trail around 9:30 AM. It was Sunday. Skies were clear, but there was a stiff breeze blowing akin to the Thursday prior. We would hike about 3 ¼ miles straight up the U-shaped valley, past Red Rock Falls, up to Bullhead Lake. That was the plan. We got started, and the gradient of the trail was pretty mellow for a while. The first 2 miles were an easy walk with understory vegetation similar to that of the Aster Park hike a few days earlier but with thinner soils. We crossed a stream early on and the trail continued up the valley toward the pass without many twists and turns. We were using our field guide to identify trees, flowers, and grasses. There was shade from the forest, but not much in the way of breeze by this point. I don't know what was more impressive, the mountains to either side of us, or the forest we were walking through. When we got close to Red Rock Falls a little short of mile 2, the trail turned from dirt to bedrock of mostly red slate and shale bedded at steep angles. There were high ridges on either side of the valley towering overhead and paralleling the trail. The rock faces were red sedimentary rocks with thin bedding planes.

Near Red Rock Falls, things got a little hairy under-foot. Vegetation was closing in from the sides, becoming ever more dense. The trail twisted around, and the bedrock was treacherous. Things turned slow-going for about half an hour. When the trail wasn't bedrock, it was mostly closed in by beargrass, thimbleberry, and service berry. There were also many cottonwoods, ponderosa pine, and limber pine trees. The first miles had more trees. The latter miles had more brushy understory. There were also plenty of pretty wildflowers the whole way through; yellow, pink, and purple. The soil was very thin, and it appeared in places that vegetation was popping up out of rocks or very rocky soil. We wanted to hike up to Bullhead Lake, but just short of the destination, we saw very fresh grizzly poop, and turned around and headed back to the car. Along the way back we saw a moose eating in Fishercap Lake, and there was a crowd of about 30 people a little more than 50 yards from the moose.

The hike at the Swiftcurrent Pass trail would be our last hike before leaving the park and heading to Yellowstone. It was a surreal day between the weather and the landscape. It was yet another dynamic pocket of that great park conditioned by its aspect to the forces of nature. The red sedimentary bedrock and vegetation growing out of rocky soil drew us in close and held us to its bosom. The shade and plant life supplemented the topography leaving a lasting impression. It released us rhythmically in a wavelength of freedom all day. The weather couldn't have been better, atmospheric conditions I would have never expected in northwest Montana. Clear skies and hot, dry air. Even the other hikers we saw on the trail imposed no negative energy. There was definitely a sense of rugged individualism as we hiked up the Swiftcurrent Pass trail that Montana August morning. The willingness to work and innocence of the hike catalyzed harmony between people and landscape. I couldn't have loved it more nor felt more in place. Knowing what I now know I do not think my life would be complete without that day and that whole week. Experiencing a place like Glacier National Park, you get a better idea of what God is capable of creating. It was so impressive that I could not conceptualize *a priori* the sights let alone the stimulation I felt in my soul before actually experiencing it. The place blew my mind.

Glacier trail log and animals seen:

8/3 Lake McDonald, Rocky Point 2.0 miles
8/4 Going to the Sun Road pull-offs and wind in Many Glacier
8/5 Two Medicine, Aster Park Trail, Running Eagle Trail 5.5 miles
8/6 Logan Pass, Hidden Lake, Trail of the Cedars 5.0 miles
8/7 Many Glacier, Swiftcurrent Pass Trail 7.0 miles

Marmot
Golden Mantled Ground Squirrel
Chipmunk
Moose
Mule Deer
Grizzly Bear
Black Bear
Bighorn Sheep
Mountain Goat
Bald Eagle

CHAPTER 8

Accommodations and the Passage from Glacier to Yellowstone

While in Glacier, we stayed at Silver Wolf Log Chalets in Coram, MT about 5 miles west of West Glacier Park, MT. The lodging was spacious, rustic, and simple. There was a comfortable bed, a small table, a full bathroom, microwave, refrigerator, coffee pot, and there were nine cabins on the grounds. The grounds spanned about 1 ½ acres and was a mix of woods, mulched walkways, and lawn. It was comfortable and romantic. We ate out for supper at the Packer's Roost all but two of the six nights there. It was pub-grub - burgers, fried fish, that sort of thing - and the beer selection was pretty good for a roadhouse. Our favorite brew on draft was Big Sky Brewing's Moose Drool brown ale. Other good beers we had during our stay in Glacier were Kettllehouse Brewing's Cold Smoke Scotch Ale and Red Lodge Ales' Czechmate Pilsner. We had lunch at the Whistle Stop in East Glacier one day where we both ordered bison burgers and huckleberry pie. The food was good and the atmosphere was relaxed. Picnic tables on a porch and modest indoor seating. It was on a little country road just outside the east side of the park. Twice we ate at the Snowgoose in St. Mary on the east side of the park. The first time at the Snowgoose, I had the best pulled-pork sandwich ever. It was topped with really good coleslaw and really good pickles. The ciabatta bun put it over the top. The second time at Snowgoose we both ordered bison burgers with goat cheese and huckleberry chutney. It was an impressive entrée. We stopped at a roadside coffee shop in Babb, MT just outside of Many Glacier near the northeast portion of the park. A roadside coffee shop was unusual to Kelly and I, but the breakfast sandwich and coffee was good, and it was rather convenient; a brilliant idea really to set up a coffee stand along a remote stretch of highway. On the trail, we munched on cliff bars, muffins, milk, and water. The muffins and milk were snagged from the continental breakfast basket supplied by our chalet. We ate good the whole time. Sometimes our resources for sustenance were a little unusual, but Kelly was getting a good look at how to fuel up while rambling. We spent a lot of time driving. Usually 2 hours in the morning and 2 hours in the evening, and on the road through the course of the day. The weather was pretty good almost the whole time. Clear, sunny skies, and daytime highs in the 90's. The air was really dry which made the heat more bearable. Between the food, weather, and terrain, we were having a great vacation. Still, we were interested in more than just the aesthetics. We were after adventure, and I was looking for answers to the question, what restores and sustains harmony? In our adventures I was discovering these things.

On Monday August 8, 2022, we left West Glacier for Butte, MT on our way to Yellowstone National Park. The landscape changed. As we passed Swan Lake on MT 83 driving south, the timber opened up a little bit. Lots of lodgepole pine and grasses. We spent two hours driving along the beautiful Montana countryside before coming to Missoula where we would get lunch at a coffee shop, and I attempted to unload some of my books in different bookstores. I was unsuccessful with the books, and the college town of Missoula had me feeling a little self-conscious. I'm not progressive. I'm open minded, but I am not liberal. I believe there is truth and goodness in tradition, every bit as much as there is goodness in progressiveness. I have learned from the Earth and the Spirit that there is more to life than what we see in this world. Immerse yourself in the natural world, and you will understand it to a higher degree. Truly immerse yourself. Take time to listen to it and let it come to you. Don't be demanding or impatient. It will only tell you its own secrets on its own time. Taking pride in being liberal is every bit as dangerous as taking pride in dogma or religion. What should be held on to are the relationships we hold, the relationships we have with each other, and the relationship we have with God. They should be held onto, but they should not be boasted about. Make an honest attempt to have etiquette, propriety, and good mannerism, but don't let these things rule what you see when you look in the mirror. Try to be the best version of yourself. Everyone can act foolishly, but stupidity should not be an acceptable status quo. Everyone has problems they're trying to work out, and we should all be able to comfort or advise anyone searching for answers, but that does not mean we should accommodate habitually making bad decisions. There is a balance between tolerating and accepting. The true purpose of tolerance is for people with different views to communicate peaceably. Arrogance is a different monster that I don't have patience for. To ask of people to patiently tolerate arrogance feels more unreasonable than patiently tolerating stupidity or foolishness.

Karma is a "get what you give" idea, and is often embraced by hip culture. I hold no opposition to karma, and even seek it out, but we should not expect to receive anything we don't earn. Good karma includes not being snobby. Open mindedness includes allowing Jesus into your heart and letting His Spirit work in your life. If you initiate a relationship with God, he will know you by name. You will be moved by His love and favor. To return His favor, be obedient. Obedience bestows blessings, and fear of eternal punishment is a good reason to be obedient to goodness. Listen first. Listen to God. That is the first step in good communication. Good communication bestows love. Love is the point of it all. Furthermore, there should be something in marriage vows about protection and patience. It is important to protect those you love from harm, but also give them enough freedom to learn from their own failures and mistakes. Wisdom and culture are passed down from generation to generation, each learning from the last. By this, culture can either improve or decline through time. I hope it does improve. I think we should all hope it improves. But, change is not something that happens instantly. It takes decades. Social behavior is learned from prior generations. Behavior is the way we treat each other and the way we treat the world around us; our success and our failures. We should look beyond superficial things, like our image, and focus on our true intentions. Be transparent. Let individually-and-communally-true intentions be known. Don't rely on image or be distracted by it. Look upon what each of our true intentions are. Focus on our true objectives. The attitude of the heart is every bit as important as any outward demonstration of perseverance. The heart-attitude toward God is every bit as important as any outward demonstration of faith.

By the time we got to Drummond, MT it was high country rangeland. More grasses than trees, and igneous rocks cropping out on the hillsides. The region looked very dry. After all, it is an arid climate. After 8/8/22 the term "arid climate" took on a new meaning for me. It wasn't desert, but it definitely wasn't the Appalachian Mountains. We passed through Anaconda, MT and I got an eerie feeling. Anaconda was a sunbaked town. Tempereatures were in the mid 90's when we passed through at 3:30 that August afternoon. Sleepy. I felt like if I stepped in any given bar there (which there was only one we passed, "Ranch Bar") some cowboys would try to beat my ass and take my girl. By the time we got to Butte, it was about 4:30 PM. We had to find a laundromat, get food, and make it to our accommodations just outside of town. Butte was another cowboy town. To be accurate Butte is a small city, bigger than a town I suppose. It had a sleepy feel, like everyone had somewhere they had to be, but lackadaisical in their progress, everyone taking a moment to look beyond themselves and accommodate for another's needs. As the 90-degree heat faded, and afternoon approached evening, we got a pizza from Pizza Hut, and made it to our cabin in Homestake just outside of Butte a little before 8:00 PM.

Homestake Lodge was serene. One of three cabins a mile or two back a dirt road in the hills above Butte, MT. The landscape and vegetation were characteristic of western Montana. Hills and valleys within the mountains, pine, and sage brush. Other conifers and brushy vegetation. Pine and grassland surrounded the cabin, and the mountains on the periphery stretched forever. The cabin was rather remote, or at least it felt that way. The interior was modern, and the structure had modern amenities: shower, stove, microwave, fridge. Comfortable bed and clean sheets. It was an incredibly relaxing and romantic escape. Not a sound could be heard from our front porch. Kelly and I just sat there enjoying the peace, and journalling as dusk cycled through. There was a feeling of untamed wilderness about the place. We hung out on the porch, full of pizza, drinking beer, and writing in our journals through evening twilight. Kelly went in to shower around 10:30, sometime after nightfall. Then and there, in romantic remoteness, Kelly and I had a passionate night.

Sensuality that will hold a premier spot in my heart and soul for all my mortal life. Such an experience came from a few places. Basing our relationship in Christian faith. Stepping out of our comfort zones. Being mindful of each other's needs. Having the insight to what the other desires. Being exclusive and empathetic of each other at all times. Innocence and the patience to see each other before we see ourselves. We made blissful love for about an hour then slipped off to sleep. I woke around 2:30 in the morning, as I often do, and stepped outside. The dark sky was absent of light pollution and the sky was bedazzled with stars. It was so impressive that I had to wake Kelly to show her the night sky. She was amazed, and set up her camera to get a picture of the stars in Homestake, Montana, grateful that I woke her. We were tucked away from civilization. It was feeding the soul.

Navigating new territory removes you from complacency. Not only must you step outside of your comfort zone, but you must execute with keen precision. Whitewater paddling has taught me a lot of that same thing. New rivers, new lines through unknown rapids, along with the possibility of losing your life if you do not execute correctly is a very fundamental practice of stepping out of one's comfort zone while navigating the unknown. Failure could result in catastrophe. That applies to most forms of competition. Economic competition is no different, removing us from complacency by the competitive spirit of survival. Furthermore, the beauty found in surviving in the wilderness is awe-inspiring and sparks feelings of freedom, both in engaging in physical activity, and the transcendental feelings that wilderness can fill you with. It puts all other experiences into a frame of reference. The demand in surviving and finding balance within competition is a matter of efficiency-versus-fairness, amongst both human resources and natural resources. How can we accommodate for fairness while being efficient with the resources we have been allocated? I will get into that later in this book, but do not be overrun with the darkness of greed. Don't let vices of luxury and convenience control your mind. Don't be blind to the value of balance or live in a depraved world.

We routed the trip from Butte to Yellowstone through a little cowboy town in Montana named Ennis. In Ennis, MT after leaving Butte on Tuesday August 9, 2022, we had trouble finding a place to eat. There were places, but all the restaurants were short-staffed. It was a good example of how crippling it can be to promote unemployment the way the government has through the course of the COVID-19 pandemic. They reduced competition thereby weakening the economy. Is it a valid question to ask whether mobility, the ability to go and adapt, or competition for a greater share of resources is of higher importance? Two things to keep in mind: 1) mobility, travel, the ability to go and adapt takes a source of funds, and 2) In both scenarios, competition and mobility, conservation is important. We must be wise in the way we use our resources.

Aside from the economics in Ennis we were immersed in the Rocky Mountains in all their majestic wonder. Huge peaks rose up off to the side of the road. Once or twice the road crawled up and over the mountains. Dry atmosphere conditioned the vegetation and landscape creating a unique environment I dreamt about all my life but never experienced until the age of 34. The drive was taken in a hazy state of mind. All day behind the wheel in such a vast expanse left me feeling an extreme sense of freedom. There weren't many towns or big neighborhoods aside from Anaconda, Ennis, Butte, and Missoula. There were ranches and smaller western neighborhoods, but the desolation satisfied my taste for adventure. Before long we would be entering Yellowstone National Park in northwest Wyoming.

CHAPTER 9

Entering Yellowstone

Yellowstone National Park covers 3,472 square miles which is over 2 million acres. We arrived through the west gate late in the afternoon on August 9, 2022. Yellowstone sits atop the biggest dormant caldera on the continent. A caldera is collapsed rock from cooled and hardened magma at the mouth of a dormant or extinct volcano. Imagine one that is over 3,000 square miles in area. Pretty big. Imagine the type of landscape that would result for such a large volcanic feature. Most of the rock in Yellowstone is either granite or basalt, which are characteristic of igneous formations. Sulfur and calcite minerals can be seen in the rock, as well as quartz, feldspar, and biotite. Obsidian, black volcanic glass, existed in nodules within the igneous rock in places. Hot springs, geysers, and fumaroles pushed superheated mineral water up by volcanic activity from below the surface of the ground. The volcanism in the park created a landscape that looked like Mars in places, and after just leaving Glacier, it was hard to appreciate such a stark contrast in beauty. Yes, there are hundreds of thousands of acres of forest and meadows, but the most unique aspect for me were the geysers and mineralogy. To say the forest took a backseat to the volcanism would be a lie. Practically unimaginable expanses of wilderness vegetation encapsulated the park in all of its wild glory. Between geothermal features and montane ecosystems this great expanse of wilderness proved to be an American gem.

When we entered Yellowstone National Park on Tuesday August 9, 2022, we came in through the west gate and approached the Madison River, one of the three major rivers that flow out of Yellowstone. The nature of the surface water in Yellowstone National Park was rather variable. There were steep shallow rivers, high waterfalls, placid sections of river with laminar flow. The rivers and streams we saw were not monotypical. The park was very wooded as one would expect, but there was a lot that could be accessed by car. Roadways and parking lots accommodated for front country tourists. Scenic views in the front country attracted many visitors, but to get greater depth, you had to venture a little further into the wilderness. As a result of well-designed accessibility features, vehicle traffic in the park was way heavier than what we anticipated. I wasn't quite sure how to compare it to Glacier at this point, but we had just arrived. The biggest contrast was probably the topography. Glacier had more steep faces and high mountain peaks. Yellowstone was more like rangeland with many volcanic features and broad and gentle slopes with grasses and trees. As we entered the park, we were blinded on the periphery by the forest. As we got down to the Madison River about ten miles east of the west gate of the park, the vegetation opened up, and a few things stood out. There were granite cliffs (igneous rock) that rose a few hundred feet above the valley floor. Some cliffs weathered and deteriorated into talus slopes. Along the valley and floodplains meadows of grasses and wildflowers cropped up, and the landscape was serene. Aside from the volcanism there were plenty of lush green forests and meadows with gently sloping mountains.

The first time I got out of the car in Yellowstone, I felt something very comfortable. It wasn't the type of comfort that facilitates complacency. It was more of a sensation that was derived from harmony. It was kind of surreal to feel such balance instantly upon arriving in the park. What brought such peace and harmony? Was it the temperature, the breeze, walking the banks of the Madison River, or the ground under foot? Was it the way the park reduced the ego such that no one would consider destroying something beautiful? It didn't feel like comfort derived from familiarity. It was something brought about by the strange and new. Was I transcending with the Spirit? After a quick stop near the Madison River, we continued on, seeing Gibbon Falls, an unrunnable 40-foot waterfall, cascading over its ledge. There were tons of people parked at the falls, checking it out from the roadside parking lot, taking pictures. The volume of tourists aggravated Kelly as it made it hard for her to get good pictures. Quietly I snickered at her disgust.

After Gibbon Falls, we moved on to Artist Paintpots, a collection of small geysers and hot springs. The water was red. The ground around the water was white. Imagine a swamp with little to no vegetation, and super-hot mineral water bubbling to the surface dissecting it with channels. The superheated mineral water smelled like sulfur. The ground wasn't completely barren, but little life existed there. Some small conifers and archea, a type of thermal bacteria that lives in the hot mineral water, inhabited the zone. It was a good representation of the mechanics of early biological evolution on Earth. It is said that a hot ooze of magma and water coalesced across the surface of Earth as it formed, similar to the conditions in these hot springs. The ooze (often referred to as organic soup) cooled and hardened, but liquid water remained in various temperatures. As the magma and water cooled, single celled organisms spontaneously generated and began to inhabit this new Earth. The environment of the organic soup with its high temperatures and high mineral concentration provided the nutrients for archea and other first ever life forms to sustain themselves. The landscape continued to evolve through differing conditions, and so did the life it supported. Separation between land and sea became evident, and the vegetation pioneered its way across these landscapes, providing food and cover for birds, fish, reptiles, and mammals. But those first environments have somehow been preserved in this pristine National Park, giving us in this current day an opportunity to see something so strange and foreign, yet so fundamental to the evolutionary history of our planet. Hints and visuals of it can be seen at many places in Yellowstone National Park. It really has the ability of provoking the imagination.

There was a weird balance I was feeling as I saw all these thermal displays of natural wonder. They weren't beautiful in the usual sense of the word, but the longer I studied these features on the landscape, the more I appreciated them, and the more impressive they became. The steam and colors of the ground presented a significance unique and intrinsic to this particular location. Maybe some of what detracted from the beauty was sharing the space with other people. The volume of tourists was higher than expected, and I began comparing the feelings of harmony I had with the landscape to the feelings of harmony between people. Harmony was not necessarily evident between people, with the exception of campers in campgrounds, but there was an element of harmony existing between individuals and the landscape.

Our nature adventures were not too far in-depth that afternoon as we still needed to eat and set up camp. We camped in Canyon Campground that first night, and it was a remedy to overwhelming population density in the park. We had no firewood, and took precautions to prevent bears getting curious with us. Once we got set up in the campground, and drank a few beers in evening twilight, we slipped into a somber rest amongst the wilds and wonders. It was feeding good vibes directly to the soul. It got cold through the night, but coffee waited in the morning with new adventures afoot.

CHAPTER 10

A New Environment

Kelly and I worked through some front country areas the first afternoon, and got a quick look at this new environment. There were some extremely beautiful and bizarre sights, and lots of people. Still, we were excited to camp for the first time on this trip. We checked into the Canyon Campground, and a ranger went over the rules and bear-safety. Then we trucked to our campsite and pitched the tent. We bought Subway sandwiches on the way in and sat at our picnic table and ate after the tent was up. I drank four beers, and we went to bed just after dark.

The tent was comfortable, although I had a little trouble with the zipper on my sleeping bag, which created a cooler sleeping environment than I would have preferred. I woke through the night a number of times, once staying up for a while. As I listened to the sounds outside of our tent, I was developing a little bit of bear-paranoia. Snoring, scratching, rumbling; all of it left me a little nervous thinking there could have been bears just outside our tent. Eventually all of that faded, and I drifted back off to sleep for a few hours.

We rose in the morning just after daybreak around 6:00 AM. I got the camp stove set up and prepared the percolator with good coffee from Montana Coffee Traders. We were in the Rocky Mountain Forest as we sat at the picnic table in the Canyon Campground of Yellowstone National Park awaiting our morning coffee. Squirrels scampered and birds sang in the lodgepole pines that populated the campground. Other campers were stirring, preparing for the day. It was a very tranquil atmosphere, but there was a good deal of excitement within both Kelly and me. The water boiled, and the coffee percolated. It was brewed. We sat in the cool 40-degree morning wearing big smiles, winter hats, jackets, layers, and long pants as we waited for the coffee to cool. It did, and we sipped. There was a dense feeling of freedom in the campground that morning. Coffee took us high, prepared fresh in the camping morning forest. The java woke the senses and energized the mind as it brought harmony between us and our environment. Jovial vitality runs through the veins and the aromatics of the brew awaken you to the natural world. Looking back at photos from the morning, we were in very good spirits. We were Yinzers in the wild. Life was good.

That morning we planned on hiking 2 miles into Cascade Lake in the western half of the park and 2 miles back to the car first thing. I didn't know what to expect from landscape, vegetation, and atmosphere. After our inception into the park the day before I was trying not to come up with any pre-conceived notions about what I was entering. I tried to keep an open mind. Looking back on it, I don't think I ever felt out of place in nature. We traveled about 10 miles of wooded roads that morning and by the time we got to the trailhead around 8:30, skies were blue and temperatures were above 65F. Hardly anyone was there. We were nervous about bears on the trail, as Yellowstone is known for an abundance of wildlife, and I tried not to let worry get the best of me. I was hoping I could enjoy the forest freely and not get preoccupied with bear-alert. We were talkative letting our presence be known, and as we progressed into the trail, bear-alert didn't feel overbearing.

The trail started through ½ mile of open forest mostly populated with lodgepole pine; tall, skinny, symmetrical pine trees. The light that filtered through the pines was beautiful, peaceful, and serene. Not much in the way of dense understory. Eventually the trail opened up to a 50+ acre meadow of yucca, chicory, monkshood, and buffalo berry; shrubs, grasses, and flowers. The mosquitos were bad, worse than I expected, and every time we came to a blind pass, I would take lead with bear-spray in hand. We had been hiking for a little over an hour, mostly on flat mountain meadow and pockets of woods. The wilderness felt as though it was sprawling. There was such an expanse of brush, grasses, and wildflowers that adventure and freedom immediately filled the head, the heart, and the feet. We couldn't completely relaxed, and soon saw fresh bear scat. Some other hikers said there was a young grizzly a ways ahead.

After crossing some dry creekbeds, and passing through some sparse woods, we saw a grizzly. He was a young boar maybe 400-500 pounds about 350 yards away at the edge of the meadow at the foot of a hill. We were less than ¼ mile away from Cascade Lake, the planned destination, and weren't sure if the bear noticed us. I wasn't taking chances. Without much panic, and after a little time to assess the situation, we turned around and headed back to the car before reaching our destination. We didn't want to continue on only to return to the bear being between us and our only way out. We hiked a little over 3 ½ miles that first morning.

The accommodating thing about Yellowstone was the ease of access by road. Roads were spread out distantly in the largest national park in the U.S. giving way to spectacular views. Most spatial relativity was lost, or not yet obtained in the vast park. Elevation was breathtaking, and most of the land was between 7,000 and 8,500 feet above sea level. Slopes were mildly to moderately steep with plenty of gentle rangeland. Watersheds spanned about 5 miles or more in width from drainage divide to drainage divide. Slopes were usually sagebrush and grassland with an almost equal amount of lodgepole pines and other conifers. The elevation, topography, remoteness, and vegetation were producing a feeling inside of me that made the trip worth every penny.

After the Cascade Lake hike we spent most of the day Wednesday August 10, 2022 driving around, and popping in on front-country views. The place was mesmerizing with a very different charm than what we had seen and felt in Glacier National Park just a few days before. Less alpine, more rangeland. I was expecting a barrage of wildlife, but instead the most abundant feature I was seeing was all the different sorts of volcanic activity. The geysers and hot springs stole the forefront as an iconic feature. I really didn't expect such a landscape. We were in Norris Geyser Basin on the afternoon of August 10th standing just above Consistent Geyser when we saw it go off twice in 5 minutes. There wasn't much warning then we saw water spewing up from underground. It was moving and personified that geology to a degree, making it feel like the edaphic features of the earth were coming to life. It was my first experience seeing a geyser erupt, and I was very moved. It was captivating and impressive. The forces of heat and pressure worked the subsurface water in an impressive fashion, but it wasn't the mechanics that impressed me the most. What impressed me the most was the possibility that such an environment and landscape could exist on this wonderful Earth. I would have never been able to conceptualize how such a place would make me feel inside before actually experiencing it. The Norris Geyser Basin was colorful with blue, pink, and white mineralogy blending across the barren landscape.

I lost myself in Yellowstone moments before Consistent Geyser went off. I was still trying to make sense of things and letting the Spirit of Yellowstone permeate through me. All the volcanic activity was not what I was expecting, but indulged in it regardless because I was there and this was what was before me. I was developing a relationship with this impressive landscape. It just seemed a bit alien. Earlier we were at Travertine Terraces where mineral water fed by hot springs deposited calcium and sulfur in terraces over the landscape. Calcite appeared in white pillowy rolls as it descended, while sulfide exhibited yellow-orange, vertical ledges. Whitebark pine and juniper grew sparsely in the silty edges of the hot springs. There wasn't much in the way of soil and vegetation at Travertine Terraces and Mammoth Hot Springs. What did exist was highly specialized and quite exotic.

After 90 minutes at Mammoth Hot Springs we moved on to Clearwater Springs, and I had a glimpse of what Native Americans might have thought of all the natural hot springs in Yellowstone while traveling through on foot before any development or contact with white people. Time and place felt mystical. There was much that would be hard to explain without deeper investigation, but still there was an ethos, pathos, and logos from the land all culminating to build a significance in the mind and soul. Clearwater Springs was a small green valley with thermal water bubbling up to the surface. The beauty of the place was not immediate or stereotypical. It was something that took a little extra time to grasp. Humbling the soul was what was required to feel harmony between the inner person and the environment surrounding you there. The hot mineral water prevented most vegetation from growing where it spread over the valley floor of Clearwater Springs some 50 yards wide. The barren landscapes in Yellowstone looked like the surface Mars at times. The aesthetic of green vegetation is easier to embrace, but the volcanic landscape was mesmerizing and full of wonder. It was a good place to experience the mystery and creativity of God's Spirit and cognize the mechanics of early evolution. It was a masterpiece of strangeness captured in time millennia ago.

CHAPTER 11

Grand Canyon of the Yellowstone River

We hiked the North Rim of the Grand Canyon of the Yellowstone River on Thursday August 11, 2022. The canyon was a vertical slot canyon that dropped hundreds of feet almost straight down from the rim to the river. It was composed of igneous geology, like other places in the park, that exhibited unique coloration and jointing. Yellow, white, and black characterized the minerology of the canyon. Quartz, calcite, and sulfur made the white and yellow that could be seen in the rocks. As we progressed into the hike, I was captivated and transcended with the Spirit along the forested ledges for the 3.2 miles of trail. Thin vegetation in rocky soil coated the landscape along the rim of the canyon. Its walls were painted in the colors of the minerals that composed it. It drew me into harmony with a landscape that was obscure and very foreign to what I am most familiar with. This was our third day in Yellowstone National Park and ninth day since we got off the train in Montana. By that point in time I had slipped into an extended moment spending quality time in the wilderness of the Rocky Mountains. Nature is like people. It appreciates quality time spent together. The more often you spend quality time with nature, the quicker you slip into harmony with its wavelengths. It only took about an hour on the trail that 12th day since we left Johnstown, PA. I was admiring the river below as we hiked. It looked like epic whitewater, but pretty inaccessible (illegal to kayak there, too). It was captivating as I watched the river crash down the mountainside, knowing fully of its power, adding to the inspiration. It humbled me and demanded respect... an incredible force that can take you to a whole other world.

The path traced the rim of the canyon where ledge met cliff, and the trail led us down its length. The vantage point was paramount. You could see the canyon, and hundreds of feet straight down to the river. Ponderosa pine grew in the silty and rocky earth. The trail dropped and rose a couple times as it crossed a few creeks along its 3.2-mile distance. Otherwise, it was generally flat. The whole time hiking in the Grand Canyon of the Yellowstone River, my wife and I were in awe and wonder. The landscape was beautiful, and I was completely impressed. It was taking me somewhere else. I never expected to see something quite as beautiful or unique in this park. The canyon walls were breathtaking where minerals peeked out. Between the color and the height of the cliffs I was very moved, to put it plainly. It was a neat experience hiking the rim of the Grand Canyon of the Yellowstone River. Even the forest felt unique and foreign as if such a forest could only exist in that particular place in those particular conditions. We were drawn in and felt harmony on a wavelength that the canyon seemed to hum along. It had its own amplitude and frequency, unique to the elevation, topography, vegetation, and geology. It was pretty cool how quickly we slipped into spiritual connection with the natural world around us that day. After almost two weeks roaming the Rocky Mountains, we were getting familiar with its frequency, and its bosom nourishing our souls.

CHAPTER 12

An Easier Day

Thursday night we slept in a cabin near Lake Yellowstone. Four walls and a bed felt nice after 2 nights of sleeping in a tent on the ground. Showering after roughing it for a couple days was also nice. Thursday evening, we spent a lot of time journaling, and we popped in the Lake Lodge for a few beers around 8:30 or 9:00. I drank two or three pints of scotch ale and had a glass of Drambuie. Kelly had a scotch ale and a glass of the same herbal, honey-blended, scotch liquor. Waking up in the cabin the next morning, Friday August 12, 2022, we decided on an easier day with less leg work. We had been putting the miles on underfoot, and I needed one day of something a little easier. We started with a hearty breakfast at the Lake Lodge and planned to see parts of the park mostly by car that day.

We drove along the shores of Lake Yellowstone in the morning sun. Skies were clear and the mountain air was crisp. Like everything else in the Rockies, Lake Yellowstone was vast. From one shore to the opposite was probably 10-12 miles or more. There wasn't much boat activity out there and the shoreline was populated with sporadic geyser basins. Catching the first breaths of the day along the waterfront felt stoic. There was much reservation in our mood, but also curiosity. The destination for both mind and body felt unknown, but our immediate location felt tranquil and satisfying; an element of mystery to whatever the objectives were ahead. Dawn was beautiful as we cruised the shores of the lake. There wasn't much tourist traffic yet, and the day was just breaking. There seemed to be an infinite collection of beauty in the vastness of Yellowstone.

We got to Gull Point, looking out over the morning waters from the shoreline, and continued on the shoreline road to West Thumb Geyser Basin. The geysers at West Thumb were modest in comparison to Old Faithful, matching some of the smaller to medium sized geysers elsewhere in the park. Water only slightly bubbled over the rims of the geyser cones, but majestic still. The ledges that sat just above the water were barren. Hot mineral water forbode anything from growing there. It was a good way to wake up. Nothing felt too strenuous as we cruised the shores and popped into a few front country features. It was nice not having to mentally prepare for adventures or spend hours on end hiking with a pack on. Relaxing as the sun climbed the sky and the air warmed made the morning feel more like vacation than exploration. Nevertheless, we explored, if only in a tame and civilized way.

By afternoon we were tromping along Sulfur Caldron and Mud Volcano geyser basins near the Hayden Valley. Once again, the landscape was dissected and inundated by hot mineral water, and the air was filled with the acrid stench of sulfur. The smell was more pronounced around Mud Volcano and Sulfur Caldron than most of the other places we had been up to that point. Murky water rose to the surface from underground bringing up minerals in solution. It created a landscape that looked like the moon, should there be water there. Some geysers gurgled, one gently roared, Dragons Mouth, a cavern in the hillside that produced mineral water.

Hayden Valley was also where we saw bison for the first time. Hundreds were there; bulls, cows, and calves. They could be seen running through gently rolling grassland next to the river, or rolling in the dust for scent marking and to keep flies off. Seeing them move about and socialize was interesting. They are so big, yet quick and powerful. Watching animals of that size gallop at speed was impressive and rather intimidating. Watching them roll in the dust with ferocity was also intimidating. Bison are the largest land animal in North America, and understandably so. Seeing them up close and in person can be described in one word: intimidating. Stoic and impressive are other adjectives that come to mind. Getting close to take selfies with these creatures looked like a terrible idea, still people were doing just that. One day we saw a bull walking down paved road with a line of cars behind him just as if he owned the road. He was roughly the size of the small bus that was behind him, maybe slightly larger. Their image and presence were iconic of untamed, American spirit.

After seeing the Yellowstone River in Hayden Valley, I got curious. I wondered about the geography of the watersheds that drained Yellowstone. I came to learn that three major rivers drain the surface water of Yellowstone National Park: The Madison River to the west, the Yellowstone River to the north, and the Snake River to the south. Another idea of interest was the fact that the geyser basins in the park produce so much water rich in minerals and high in temperature that the rivers they flowed into must hold very unique and specialized ecosystems.

When considering the development and function of all we saw, one has to consider the fundamental elements that build up to compose the sum of these parts. Each factor in composition conditions the products they create, whether those factors are our genetics or the chemistry of the Earth. Does God set limits through genetics? God will define limits according to His will of altruism and compassion. He is the God of love, strength, and goodness. Love is facilitated through beauty. Strength is found in sacrifice. Sacrifice warrants appreciation and gratitude. Some are never thanked for the sacrifices they make, never nurtured. Some are just plain out abused or neglected. The scope of who the abused are can appear a little vague or obscure sometimes. That can adjust the way you feel love or show love. Some people need love in ways others don't understand. Be handsome. Validate those around you and those you come across as best you can; even include them in your lives. Why make someone feel like an outcast? Loneliness is one of the worst feelings in the world. Fellowship. Develop community. Sometimes fellowship and survival-mode *aren't* the same thing. Sometimes fellowship and survival-mode *are* the same thing. Surviving a tyrant might mean you and your fellows have to run from the authorities, but why would we have to run from forces that are just, not tyrants? That might take a degree of empathy. I think we all want others to see things our way. I think that's part of the human condition. Trying to see things the way of someone else aids in harmony. If we put ourselves in someone else's shoes, we can better understand their struggles and appreciate the strength it took to overcome the challenges they faced. Is there a greater consciousness controlling the habits of life? The habits of landscape? Is there a set code that can be tracked through the evolution of time? Genetics and chemistry are a code of habit and can place limits on life and landscape; a quick and dirty explanation of minimums and maximums. Can it tell of where we're headed or where you're coming from? You can't dwell too much in one direction, but it's healthy to reflect and ponder on both source and destination. After sensing places like Glacier and Yellowstone, I'm a firm believer that, through communing with the Holy Spirit, the Spirit of Creation, we can transcend our limits, taking risks, and stepping out of our comfort zones. Shock-factor adds little depth to our character. The ability to negotiate unseen-and-intense are a shock to the senses, too. They build character and place no burden on bystanders.

Both character and genetics are conditioned by the environments that God has created. This conditioning allows mutations to propagate through time in an effort to adapt, or else we are erased from existence. Adaptation is a matter of 'becoming' as we are transformed to negotiate our surroundings, as God has created both it and us. These becoming-changes occur subtly through long periods of time and have the ability to track us through a lineage tracing back through family history. If you believe in grand design, maybe genetics are a way for the Almighty to track down individuals and assign them specific works of His will, and specific character of their nature. Not because those works or our nature are what we are familiar with, but because of the cloth we have been cut from. Still, heritage is not nor ever will be synonymous with salvation. No matter the purpose of genetics, technical or abstract, living and edaphic features have the ability to transcend beyond what we conceive as our limits. Limitations do not define creation. God is infinite. Greater definition is given to our spiritual lives when we transcend limits. How can we sustain a fulfilling spiritual life? Righteousness, fairness, and honesty lay the groundwork of sustainability. If we embrace honesty, fairness, and righteousness, our differences mean little in the pursuit of harmony. We all come from a single source, the same source that also gave definition to both us and our world, assigning an ethos, pathos, and logos through the continuum of time, space, and matter. Spontaneous generation and the supernatural filter down through the matrix of creation, tracing things from start to finish, and exposing a pool of elements from that primal starting point. Divergence from habit as energy and consciousness progress creates variety. Disturbance provides an opportunity for new characters (strength within variation) to establish dominance. To what end is the use of dominance? Variety enriches the world. Undulating cycles of energy and consciousness between elements of creation must be harmonized. Altruism and love will propagate. The cyclic flux allows all of creation to diverge in strange directs. Sometimes for the benefit. Sometimes to disadvantage.

In Yellowstone and Glacier, awe, wonder, and inspiration exceeded anything I might have experienced or conceptualized before, at least in a positive way. I was transcending the habits I was limited by prior to this trip. I was now in a new ecosystem. The landscape was foreign with only slight prior insight. The thermal features and geyser basins in Yellowstone created a landscape I had not anticipated. The peaks and topography of Glacier transcended beyond anything I could have conceived prior. At no point was I disappointed with what I traveled to witness. It was an experience I can hold all others relative to. Lake Yellowstone let on a divinity of infinity. The lake, especially in those morning moments, was evidence that limits do not define life. We are only limited by our perception, and God will give us the power to become anything that He wills, and you are willing to pursue.

It is evident that with God, anything is possible. The creatures of the Hayden Valley, and the valley itself, were a canvas painted by the beauty of God's hand. It was evidence of God's love for beauty. Get close to bison and you will agree; beautiful, enormous creatures. The world of Yellowstone National Park was certainly a wild and untamed place. The visitors did not lessen this. If anything, that was confirmation that many people on this Earth have an attraction to such wilds and find fulfillment in adventuring in such places. Being there was a great privilege. The hard work my wife and I put into this living paid us a trip to truly great places. It might have been more than we deserved, but grace and hard work got us there. That privilege was extended by the great freedom our forefathers established in making the United States of America. It felt like foresight into the future gave us freedom to roam such a wild place as the future became present.

CHAPTER 13

Fairy Falls and Grand Prismatic Lake

On Saturday August 13, 2022, we parked at the Fairy Falls trailhead, and planned to hike past Grand Prismatic Lake back to Fairy Falls. The overlook to the lake was less than a half mile beyond the trailhead. Getting out that morning, we had the mountain air in our lungs. The forest and meadows that bordered the Firehole River coaxed us to pursue yet another day of the Rocky Mountain wilds. At this point, we were 14 days into our trip. I was wondering how my endurance would hold up. Early mornings and roving long distances for such a duration of time left me wondering if at any point I'd call it quits and mope, or drag ass until our return home. That never seemed to happen, but I had to control impulses of becoming impatient. Also, as time progressed, my decision making adjusted, veering towards efficiency above all else. We had a pretty good view of Grand Prismatic Lake from the Fairy Falls trail, though it was kind of off in the distance. Kelly was not satisfied and wanted eventually to get closer for pictures, just maybe not that same day. We could see vapors rising to the heavens and minerals left behind. Hot water at the center of the hot spring exhibited an impossible shade of blue, and colors graded out through the spectrum of visible light as you approach Grand Prismatic Lake's edges. The center is blue from the hot water (188F) refracting blue wavelengths of light that are not absorbed, but the greens, yellows, and reds that could be seen in the water were produced by thermophiles, bacteria living in the hot mineral water. As water flows over the edge of the pool, a thin layer flows overground with a crust of bacteria at the bottom, and an ice-like glaze is visible at the surface. The only feature in the park I saw that could match the beauty of Grand Prismatic Lake was the Grand Canyon of the Yellowstone River. But even that was like comparing apples to oranges. I was lost in the majesty and variety of ecosystems and landscapes produced by the caldera Yellowstone sat upon.

The Fairy Falls trail was intriguing and even a bit forgiving. As we moved past the lake, I was smelling beach scents from the water and minerals. We entered pine forest where burn-revegetation by lodgepole pine was thick, so thick in places it did not appear large animals could move through. However, there were game trails that passed through the forest. It was some of the densest forest I've ever walked through. The topography was flat as it passed along the base of the mountain. After about 1 ½ miles of walking through, the forest thinned, and a meadow opened where the mountain formed a cliff. A spraying spout of water dropped roughly 100 feet down to the ground we were standing on, Fairy Falls. Fairy Falls was a quiet, exclusive escape.

Other hikers were there but it was not nearly as crowded as the front country, maybe 20-30 people around. I took a moment to decompress beneath the rocky outcrop and the falls, as Kelly snapped a few pictures.

Later in the day, we visited Black Sand Geyser Basin which had a somewhat substantial geyser erupting rather frequently among other hot springs and geysers. The basin spanned about 5 acres, the average size of the geyser basins we were seeing in Yellowstone. The geyser basins were alien, and I had a hard time admiring them. I connected some kind of mystical wavelength to them, but it was something obscure, and rather strange. They were mostly barren ground with white and pale-yellow mineralization as hot mineral water flowed out over the surface. Smoke rolled out of the ground, and water sprayed above the surface. Eventually I found charm in the geysers akin to a strangeness you couldn't help but love. Luckily, I had no expectations about most of what I was seeing. Maybe it was better that way. I was forced to let these thermal features move over me and let their spirit mold an honest impression, far more valuable than anything I could conjure in the mind, *a priori*. Mysticism is what was purveyed most dominantly.

Around lunchtime we saw Old Faithful erupt. If you don't know anything about this geyser, it is the icon of Yellowstone; a geyser, the largest active geyser in the park, and it erupts at such a regular frequency that it has earned its name. On that day, eruptions were charted to occur every 91 minutes, plus or minus ten minutes. To have such regularity, you need a few things: a constant volume of water, a constant storage volume, and constant temperature influence to heat the water causing it to expand and pressurize. More or less like a tea kettle, when the water gets hot enough, out the spout it comes. Once erupting, it shot water 75 feet or more in the air. It went off in multiple bursts for a total of roughly 90 seconds. I was surprised how long the eruption went on. I was moved by the experience. I'm not sure what I was expecting to sense, but whatever it was, the experience exceeded that. The size and power of Old Faithful laid at the root of what impressed me. The whole thing looked both hostile and amazing. To think the same forces that made Old Faithful also made the whole human race is a humbling experience. Waiting to see the eruption, we sat on the deck of one of the lodges just after eating lunch in the cafeteria inside. The atmosphere was very relaxed. The 25 minutes we waited for the eruption was passed by talking to a hip middle-aged couple from Oregon. We shared stories about whitewater kayaking and skiing, then boom! The water blew high into the sky. We were astounded for an eternal 90 seconds. I will always remember seeing that water go high into the sky.

Late in the day, we took a drive up Firehole River Canyon. Firehole River is the second largest river in the Madison River watershed. Like the rest of the park, it is cut out of granite. It probably pushes 1,500 cubic feet per second of water through its lower reaches. Midway Geyser Basin, which holds Grand Prismatic Lake, drains into this river. Up in the canyon, there is some epic whitewater. While driving around Grand Loop Road in the afternoon with rain clouds building, we stopped at the Chief Joseph/Nez Perce War of 1877 roadside exhibit. The Nez Perce are a Native American tribe of the Northern Rocky Mountains. Native American culture has always fascinated me, especially the Nez Perce, or their name in their own language, "Nimipu" or "people". The tale of the war was heart breaking as it depicted how the U.S. army ran the tribe off their home territory despite the Nimipu putting up a valiant fight. Col. John Gibbon led U.S. forces and appears to have made a name for himself fighting Native Americans after his time fighting for the Union Army in the Civil War. I'm not sure what destiny was to be manifested in the pioneer age, but running Natives off their homeland did not seem applicable. Banding together with close minded notions feels archaic in today's age. Back then it seemed more common to only be accepting of people like ourselves. Maybe, maybe not. Open-mindedness has been built, among other things, through the civil rights movement, and great people like Dr. Martin Luther King Jr. and all his affiliates. They ought to be more accredited and appreciated for social progress in this country's history. There has been real progress made in civil rights since those days, no matter if the state is trying to convince us otherwise. Be grateful for the progress and thankful for people like them. The world for minorities in this country is better today than it was 100 years ago, and you would have a hard time convincing me or anyone from that era otherwise.

As we left Firehole River Canyon, we headed east toward the continental divide and further on to our campground in Grant Junction. Rain was moving in, and we were getting a little lackadaisical late Saturday afternoon. We made it to Craig Pass where the road crosses the continental divide. We sat there in desolation, postponing setting up camp for the night. Rain was picking up as we watched a mother duck and some ducklings in a hilltop pond beside a pull-off along the road. As we sat there watching the duckies in the rain, a man on a bicycle was taking shelter. He was riding across the country, starting in Astoria, Oregon, peddling through heavy rain that afternoon. The vegetation was dense and lush, dripping with vibrant color. It was a very somber moment. It felt like the car, the mountain, and the rain were all we had.

We arrived at our campground in Grant Junction on Saturday around 6:15 PM and bought a box of firewood at registration with rain clouds impending. My wife Kelly and I pitched the tent quick enough to not have rain pour on us before the rain-fly was attached. We ate cold sandwiches in the car while thunder and lightning fired for about 2 hours. I didn't want to be in the car, but Kelly was fearful of the electrical storm. Finally, I talked her into migrating to the tent. Once nestled in, we joked and snuggled while drinking beer. Kelly didn't take me seriously when I told her that camping in conditions such as that is best spent inside the tent, drinking. I don't know if she underestimated the fun and coziness of that situation, but she had little confidence in the tent providing protection from the elements. Retreating to stiffer protection might have been in her mind's eye, but I was thinking of something cozy. The closeness of two people up and alert inside a tent during harsh weather coaxes the heart in a jovial direction. The beer needed drank, and we needed to be happy. To me, those things could only be done from inside our tent. Once she finally agreed to join me, we sat in there on our sleeping bags at dusk sipping beer. The closeness we felt within the shelter brought laughter and joy in a way we had not shared before. We were having a really good time for awhile. It rained hard enough and long enough that our campground was inundated with water. After the beer was all drank, we journey to the bathroom. When we returned, Kelly noticed the inside of the tent was absorbing dampness from underneath. Neither of us wanted to sleep in wet sleeping bags. Even the fire pit was filled with water. I was hoping to light a fire to lift our spirits and keep us warm, dry, and jolly for a few hours through the night, but now, even that was impossible. So, we slept in the front seats of the car Saturday night. That was not great. But the cozy moments drinking beer in the tent while it was raining was something both Kelly and I could hold onto.

CHAPTER 14

Regrets and Clearer Views

When we rose a little before dawn on Sunday August 14, 2022, to what was supposed to be our last full day in Yellowstone, last night's rain had me considering leaving early. The news saddened Kelly. As I was making coffee on the camp stove and percolator, I noticed all the surface water that accumulated the night before had now completely infiltrated into the ground. I didn't know what I wanted to do in the aftermath. We had reservations in another campground for Sunday night, but there was a chance of rain, and I didn't want to spend another miserable night sleeping in the car.

Quickly, we broke down camp and headed to Midway Geyser Basin before parking filled up to get a closer view of Grand Prismatic Lake. We arrived at 8:30 AM and there wasn't much parking left. You could sense the sun trying to pierce through and burn off the fog atop the mountain on that damp morning in Yellowstone. The rain from the night before left the ground and vegetation saturated and glistening. It was the only heavy rain we experienced on the entire trip. Midway Geyser Basin was filling up quickly. It was probably the premier geyser basin in the park, despite Old Faithful drawing a larger crowd, and Norris Geyser Basin having a similar magnitude of features. There was so much going on in Midway Geyser basin, which spanned about 10-acres. It was super dynamic. Many fumaroles and pools of thermal water. A boardwalk spanned the basin, and as we walked its length, we saw craters of extinct geysers that could, at one time, rival Old Faithful, one of which was Excelsior Geyser. Excelsior Geyser was said to have as frequent and more intense eruptions than Old Faithful before it had gone extinct. The valley was foggy from the rain making the thermal features hard to see. Our first two loops through the basin, we couldn't see the beautiful colors emanating from the hot spring because of the steam generated by 40F air hitting 188F water. We did 2 loops around the basin and went back to the car to wait for the steam to clear so we could get a clearer view and Kelly could get better pictures.

Around 10:45 AM we hiked back up the hill to see if conditions improved. They were better but not prime. Most of the fog had moved out of the geyser basin, but there was still steam hovering over Grand Prismatic Lake preventing a clear view or a clear snapshot. We sat next to a British couple our age and chatted with them until they left around 11:20 AM. Kelly and I hung around another 15 minutes before hunger got the best of us. Just before we left, a shade of impossible blue could be seen through the steam with green and yellow spreading out to the edge of Grand Prismatic Lake.

In early afternoon we checked into Madison Campground. The skies were clear, and the weather was pretty warm, so we tried our hand at curing all the moisture problems our tent absorbed the night before. We unpacked the tent and wiped everything down with a towel, then set up the tent. The bright sun and the 75-80F temperatures seemed to be a good solution to our problem. We left the campground in midafternoon and headed down South Entrance Road around 3:30. South Entrance Road takes visitors through the most remote section of the park with the least accessible features covering over 1,500 square miles. We passed Lewis Lake and sat on its black sand beaches of weathered basalt. We peered out over the lake and zoned out for about 15 minutes, allowing the vastness of the lake to draw out any stress or confusion that laid in our minds. The lake was vast, but small compared to Lake Yellowstone. Light rain fell with clear skies behind. We headed a little further down South Entrance Road until we came to Lewis Falls, a large cascade pouring out from the lake. Unfortunately, we could not get close to the cascading waterfall due to bridge construction, quite possibly from the 500-year-floods that hit the park that spring. Roads were washed out severely, and there was damage all over the park that workers were trying to recover from.

Another limitation from damage done by spring flooding that year was that the Lamar Valley was closed off in the northeast region of the park. I was a little disappointed we didn't get to drive through the Lamar Valley and maybe even hike a little bit. That part of the park is said to be the best for viewing wildlife. The wildlife prospect of such a great park was captivating. I romanticized a little about witnessing creatures endemic to the central Rocky Mountains. Heading south down the road, the Grand Teton Mountains could be seen off in the distance, pulling our imagination into deeper wanderlust.

With the tent a bit dryer and the forecast changed to clear skies for the night, Kelly and I camped in Madison Campground Sunday night. I built a fire for the first time on the trip, and we bought a six pack of craft beer at the general store in Madison Campground. We stayed up until about 11:00 PM and took in the feels of the last night we would have in Yellowstone. It was a nice feeling, very calm. The weather helped us relax as did the beer, and temperatures dropped dramatically through the night. Five days in Glacier National Park and six days in Yellowstone National Park accumulated to an ethos of a reverent moment Sunday Night. The mountain-west was pulsating in our veins with a calm, harmonious rhythm. The landscape, flora, fauna, and atmosphere imparted spirit onto us that couldn't be duplicated. After the trip, I couldn't imagine never having this experience. I don't think it took anything extraordinary to pull off, just cooperation and motivation. We escaped post-pandemic realities and immersed ourselves in the landscape and ecology of the Rocky Mountains for 13 days. The last night in Yellowstone was somber punctuation to our grandest adventure together. Things wild had become commonplace, and as I gazed at the flames and felt the warmth of our fire that night, I felt a newness and a reckoning as a result of testing my wits and endurance. We stepped out of our comfort zone and pursued the grandest of freedoms. The beer tasted ever so sweeter. I crawled in the tent after enjoying a few brews and slipped off to a satisfying sleep. I woke up around 4:00 in the morning to pee and it was frigid for summer outside the tent, temperatures around 35F. Unexpectedly, the tent stayed relatively warm inside. We rose around 6:20 AM Monday August 15, 2022, made coffee, broke down camp, then left the park.

Yellowstone National Park was spectacular. The wildlife, geyser basins, Grand Canyon of the Yellowstone River, mineral deposits, and vast mountain ecosystems built an aura of the mountain-west that will remain in our hearts forever. We drove from Yellowstone National Park in Wyoming to Butte, MT that

Monday where we stayed the night in the center of town. Passing along the country roads from northern Wyoming into southwest Montana, there were not many guardrails or road signs, allowing the beauty of the region to shine through the landscape. The Northern Rockies never failed to amaze me.

Yellowstone trail log and animals seen:

8/10 Cascade Lake 3.5 miles
8/11 North Rim Trail 6.5 miles
8/12 Front Country Views
8/13 Fairy Falls 5.0 miles
8/14 Midway Geyser Basin 1.0 mile

Badger
Grizzly Bear
Bison
Elk
Mule Deer
Coyote
Squirrel and Chipmunk
Marmot
Bald Eagle

CHAPTER 15

Conclusion

You could see the diversity of the visitors in the park. Many of those in Yellowstone National Park appear to come from the city or suburbs. Not all appear to be the rugged outdoorsy type. On the surface, they do not appear to be people who are very deliberate about communing with nature or have much of a habit for it. Nevertheless, they were drawn to these great wilds just the same. Each and every one of us need places like Glacier and Yellowstone; places to reconnect to the natural world. Maybe we need this connection more than we all realize. Maybe we need to get to reality more often. Technology and entertainment hold precedence in the lives of people in this country. In America, we have gotten very good about developing ways to entertain ourselves. Sports, movies, music, cell phones, video games. It all distracts us from things that matter the most. But what of those things? What of nurturing the soul? What of the value of things that build character and sustain harmony? The value of good communication? Being able to relate to others puts us in a kinder position, one where the way we perceive ourselves and the way others perceive us is most accurate to where we truly are in life. These wilds are places to develop communication, between the landscape and the people around us. They might even help us tolerate people we disagree with and convict our hearts of divine values. They give the most common people an opportunity to escape on a transcendental level...The deepest sense of God's handiwork. When communing with nature, the mechanics and amazing wonder of God and the Holy Spirit become evident. Observation and reflection pay great dividends, bringing us closer to a sense of love. Love must be sensed, but there are different ways of communicating love. Universal truth helps us love in the spirit of Christ. Things like being honest and fair, having a good heart attitude towards God, and inherently being made in God's image of love and strength. God created. Jesus is messiah. We are all sinners. This is what appears to me as universal truth. We have been blessed with much. Disrespect towards what we have been blessed with is the same as taking advantage of people and landscape. The hand that once nourished is now the hand that punishes. Beauty and sacrifice are probably the greatest lesson that engaging with nature can teach, elements of love and strength. Beauty and sacrifice are elements within the human spirit that sustain us as a race. Beauty facilitates love. Sacrifice is love in action. The *world* is a reflection of the human spirit. And with a little reflection, we begin to connect with the natural forces that create and condition all we have been blessed with.

Conditioning and influence amongst communities is reflected from our environment back onto us. The self is a reflection of the world, and the world is a reflection of the self. The vibe from the world around us has the ability to either fill us with burden or freedom. This is not always evident. God works in mysterious ways and mysteries lay in wait in nature for us to explore. Nature has ways of fulfilling us in ways most other things can't. Despite needing a connection to nature, we should always remember that there is more to life than what we see in this world. Too much *focus* on the landscape while ignoring the direction the world and its people can skew priorities. Too much *detachment* from it can lead to delusions and greed. Jesus said the most important commandment was to love God and love people. Enlightenment about this world and the next can be gained by communing with the natural world, but we cannot ignore God and/or ignore the people around us. Even God pays attention to environmental justice and social equity. Higher direction exists within a righteous, spiritual mind, and the holiness of God fuels a calling to transcend the bounds of this earth. With a little understanding and the right eyes, conclusions can be made about nature and the supernatural. It ebbs and flows in wavelengths, wavelengths we can fall in sync with. The heart attitude about the Creator and His Creation are ever important in finding and sustaining that harmony. When we deviate from respect and gratitude, we are taking wonder and grace for granted. We become detached from what is most natural, love. We should see the world with the innocent eyes of a child, and discipline ourselves to become patient enough to sense nature's wavelengths, moving in time with them. We harmonize through sacrifice of impulses. Soft Hearts will appreciate the beauty before them, and hard hearts will be softened.

We find challenges within ourselves, and we find challenges presented from the world around us. One can teach us about overcoming the other. Diversify. Nature can assimilate our challenges while keeping individuality in our character, and with a little self-discipline, it can level the playing field. We just have to take the time and initiative to engage. Fight the elements and terrain to obtain the treasures deep beneath the surface or way up in the high country. It will give us a more honest identity and remind us of how similar we truly are, things that are righteous to pursue. Our identity should not be based on personal truths. They should be based on universal truth: honesty, fairness, and the heart attitude toward God. Personal truth? There is no justification for a reality-network woven completely around personal truths. Values of patience, humility, sacrifice, and hard work reveal themselves in such places as these. God can make all things beautiful, including the smelly, ugly brute that was once myself. If we demand honesty, fairness, and transparency, could we develop a vital identity and honest representation of our real selves?

Society and politicians have no upper hand in these wilds, just as they shouldn't be able to decide who our real selves are and what our identity in the Creator is. These wilds restore our identity. And for the greatest degree of inner pleasure things are done well for the sake of doing them well. A good cup of coffee. Clean water and fertile soil. We take satisfaction in a job well done. That is what will produce the most good to the most people. No one is looked past or stepped on in a system that incorporates conservation and balance. Maybe politicians should be paid a living wage and not an affluent wage to understand the means by which the working class, the people they represent, live. Maybe they should be more honest and more transparent. What you put into something is often close to what you get out of it. Waste not. Nature has the ability to teach about courage, positivity, and satisfaction. It seems counter intuitive to think that by distancing ourselves from society and placing ourselves in seclusion, we can improve our ability to communicate, but with the clarity that you gain in communing with nature, all forms of communication improve. In these remote wilds communication is purely awesome.

On our train ride home, the Amtrak attendant for our sleeper car was a black man named Manny. We were not in nature, but in an environment that had the ability to condition our consciousness. Manny was very charismatic and had very good work ethic. He seemed to enjoy his job. He made our train ride from Montana to Chicago very enjoyable. He worked hard to make sure the whole car was happy and comfortable the whole time. And even if things weren't going his way, he did it all with a smile. He had a knack for seeing beyond himself. He had great character. I asked him if the company compensates him well, and he said they do. There are people who won't soften their hearts to diversity in today's day and age, but I think, generally, most of us are working toward fairness and inclusion. Those who are not, their nature is their misfortune. No one should be alienated for things that are outside of their control. No group of people should be disrespected because of being born into a type of group. It felt as though all the time and effort from Dr. Martin Luther King Jr. and the civil rights movement put forth really did make a difference in today's living conditions, opening our eyes to equality, the human condition, and good communication. A man is not an island. We must harmonize with each other and the world around us. We must be humble before God.

PART II

Government, Liberty, and Justice

INTRODUCTION

To complement the transcendental values from experiencing Glacier and Yellowstone, I paralleled the first part of this book with logic and rationale that approach topics of tyranny and injustice in this second part. By doing this I combine experience and theory to form an application of values. Might they resound the goodness within government, liberty, and justice supporting well-ordered society in a way that we can trust and rely on our fellow humans. Hopefully they will inspire us to reflect on the relationship between the self and the world around us. In this second part, I studied five philosophical works. They were some of the more prominent, politically geared philosophy books I have come across in recent times. Some of which, merging religious ideology with political ideology, and not always in ways we might expect. Each one of these has focal points that help develop a more thorough view of freedom; freedoms we hold, both as individuals and part of a society. I read these works in the same year Kelly and I took our trip to Glacier and Yellowstone. By paraphrasing each one I pulled the most relevant information from each. They give a general scope of the roles and responsibilities of both government and citizens and help define morality and righteousness. There is wisdom in each that can be used to shape a better world. Might we extend these ethics to build more sound societies, communities, and habits. May we find the strength to endure this world and make good decisions to pave the way for a bright, beautiful future.

The first of the five I reviewed is John Locke's "Second Treatise of Government" which focuses on the role and responsibilities of government. The responsibilities were examined in government's relationship with their people and spends a lot of time defining states of war, states of nature, and

101

the rights to peace and protection. It was written in 17th century England. The second is John Stuart Mill's "On Liberty" which focuses on the value of liberty and how liberty enriches the culture of a nation. It approaches the usefulness of free-thinking and places greater value on passion and impulse than dogma and etiquette. It was written in 19th century England. The third is John Rawls' "A Theory of Justice" which was written in America in the mid-20th century. As the title states, it gives good grounds for the principles needed to build a good framework of justice amongst societies. It talks about expressing our nature in ways to strengthen well-ordered society from a bottom-up approach where everyone has equal citizenship and equal opportunity. "A Theory of Justice" has the feel of the civil rights movement of mid-20th century America. It is lengthy, but has sound logic. The fourth selection I summarized was William J. Federer's "Socialism: The Real History from Plato to the Present." It focused on the real effects of socialism, which often leads to communism, written sometime after the height of the Corona Virus pandemic of the 21st century. This one felt very traditional, patriotic, and conservative, but provided great evidence to support his claim. The final piece I examined for this part of the book was "Truth over Tribe: Pledging Allegiance to the Lamb, Not the Donkey or the Elephant" co-authored by pastors Keith Simon and Patrick Miller. It was very insightful in assigning moderation to our political attitudes. This book explained how the divisiveness used by politics and most forms of media can be defused by holding allegiance to a more inclusive tribe, the tribe of King Jesus. Hopefully these summaries will open your eyes to new ways of thinking, and give cognitive diversity grounded in truth and logic. Hopefully you disagree with at least one thought here, verification that you are thinking for yourself. Hopefully you agree with at least one thought here because cooperation and respect will get you further than skill and talent ever will.

CHAPTER 16

John Locke, "Second Treatise of Government"

In 17th century English philosopher, John Locke's, "Second Treatise of Government," Locke presents the purpose of government, and elaborates on how certain features of government are supposed to function. It was written in England in the 1600's around the beginning of the Age of Enlightenment. By today's standards, it's not extremely progressive. However, it does accuse corrupt forces for developing and sustaining dysfunctional systems. Blame is not explicit. Locke works to outline basic rights for those who remove themselves from states of nature and consent to live under government. He works at explaining the purpose and obligation for a man who removes himself from a state of nature and submit to a sovereign governing body. He also talks about the duty governing bodies are responsible for. In a state of nature, however, people face numerous dangers, among them health and safety. In submitting to government, people are allotted numerous freedoms, among them, protection of natural rights and living on an agreed set of rules. People who place themselves under a governing force gain theses rights and protections of their specific commonwealth. The commonwealth supplies equal and known rights, as well as efforts to protect people from a state of war. This is the government's primary purpose. War defined by Locke is not always international warfare as we know it today, but rather a state of aggression inflicted by one person onto another, and also people against people.

He starts by searching for purpose of government. Locke explains the scope and purpose of civil government, political bodies, fellowship, community, and the order in which individuals in those realms hold power over one another. Power and judgement are to be administered justly. No man can judge himself justly. In judging himself any man would show himself too much mercy causing biased decisions and convictions. This sets limits of who can judge whom, and states no one, *not even leaders*, are right to judge their own actions. Judgement should be impartial and unbiased. Deviation from this sense of justice creates abuse of power, and abuse of power can put us in a state of war or contempt, possibly between subjects and leaders, where one person or people are aggressing upon another person or people. Government is in place to protect people from a state of war that would otherwise develop with no protection in a state of nature, should they remain in a state of nature. A state of war is not natural. This is an important distinction. In a state of nature, people live peacefully, and protect themselves and their property out of necessity, in any way they deem acceptable, when they are aggressed upon. In war, however, there is force without right from the aggressor unto the innocent. Protection and redress are necessary for the innocent by unbiased application of law. Protection and redress of the innocent are upheld by the government when people place themselves under the governing body of a commonwealth. The innocent should be the ones to reap the greatest benefits of placing themselves under government. Unbiased application of the law affords the innocent the rights and protection that were agreed upon when the government was set in place. There must be retribution towards those who attack the innocent. There is not always one who can judge the actions of an aggressor, so ultimately, when there is no judge on Earth, the appeal goes to God in Heaven.

This demonstrates how obedience bestows blessing. By following the rules, we are able to get the most out of society. This also means the rulers of society are to play by the rules with responsibility, morality, and must not take advantage of those they rule over. Locke raises the question as to what causes aggression. Greed and prejudice might override our intentions and better judgement causing villains to attack the innocent. Then, no longer we reap the benefit of community. Altruism and morality are given up in aggression and it is now the government's responsibility to restore a wavelength of harmony. In removing us from a state of nature, the government takes on a responsibility to act to preserve our wellbeing and protect us from any situation that places us in a state of war.

Locke moves on to the ideas of slavery and property, stating slavery is a continuation of the state of war. A lack of compensation for time, effort, and resources is a state of war. When there *is* reparation for sacrifices given, we are not in a state of war. When there is payment for goods and services, we are not in a state of slavery and we are not in a state of war. When there is no payment for goods or labor, we have taken that which we do not deserve. Slavery is taking away that which we have no right to take away.

According to Locke, property is marked by the labor expressed upon resources. If we are able to put work into the land to generate more value, then the land and its products are now ours. Now I ask, what is the true value of the land? It is more than its production towards industry. There are *intangible* values for our own good derived from nature. There is value in how we might be able to manage the land and resources for inputs to the community, such as farming and timber, but value can also be generated by merely spending time in nature. Furthermore, the land is ours to steward, and is a reflection of ourselves, God, and how we fit in the world around us. Land management can give us purpose as stewards of the natural world. Land can be doubly managed, or a place where we spend quality time. With a purpose of keeping it in great condition, the land reflects human's duty to God, our environment, and ourselves. Locke would argue that by cultivating wilderness, land can become 10-100 times more valuable to its people (by the goods it produces). This can be true. Our natural resources have been created for us to utilize, and by utilizing them, we have built great societies. Its resources are constantly being used to perpetuate healthy, safe, and comfortable ways of life. But it is also true that landscape in its original state is valuable. So, we must find balance in the name of conservation. Locke also claims that when a person has gathered more than he can use before it spoils or is of excess, he has stolen from his fellow countryman. This is an embodiment of conservation. Harmony demands that we do not take more than we need. Furthermore, when we take more than we need, we exceed our rights to the fruits of the land, taking away from others who rightly deserve the resources. Still, competition exists, and not always in a sporting way. When we get so driven to acquire the most and have luxurious lives, we lose sight of conservation and equality. There is a balance that must be achieved, and it extends from seeing beyond ourselves. We must be mindful and listen to and act in benefit of the needs of those around us. Not just for our own gain. Greed will breed hostility. Both of which are sins.

Locke speculates on man's consent under government in agreeing to the use of money. He builds his argument that the value of land is a result of its usefulness and the commodities it produces. And, the commodities it produces can be shared with compensation so others can enjoy the resources in a way that can accumulate something of value that does not perish as quickly. When we disconnect the use of money from the usefulness of the land, we get less hung up on the reserves we bank, and we accommodate for more morality in society and government. Still society has become very dependent on money, money mostly generated by the goods and services provided by our resources. Its need and use are hard to get away from. Hoarding resources is dishonest. By the use of money, we can hoard something more versatile and less perishable, having a usable value at some point into the future. In the notion of procurement for the future we can lose sight of the wellbeing of others. Truly, if our brothers and sisters are better off in their condition, then the rest of the world, including ourselves, is in a better condition, too.

Locke presents the order of paternal (family) law, stating that both the mother and father have equal power over the children, and with the growth in both age and reason, power over the children loosens until children are fully grown. Ability and understanding grow in a person as they mature. Hopefully they have been conditioned to live in an obedient and harmonious way, growing through their years. Knowing the law and acting within its boundaries is wise and shows maturation with obedience and harmony. It puts the law at our dispose. In this way the law is for our benefit and not our hinderance. Locke draws a difference between paternal power and political power. In paternal power there is the ability to bestow an inheritance upon children. And to enjoy an inheritance of the land, the child must take on the same terms of whichever commonwealth the land exists in, and their ancestors were under. As values are built within a commonwealth, richness of the nation can be enjoyed by the generations that pass through in time. Locke leans toward the notion that there is no one better to govern us as youngsters than our father, and even as we become adults, the best to govern us is our own family and its older generation. Through the thought that wealth accumulates through generations, heredity of kingdoms is too easily taken away from fathers and handed over to political authorities in a commonwealth. "...princes be priests since it is as certain that in the beginning the father of the family was priest as that he was ruler in his own household."

Traditional family situations are examined where one man marries one woman and they raise children together. Locke explains that the reason men and women mate for life might be because one child of theirs might not be ready to set out on their own before subsequent children are born. Also, us humans, through the great Creator, have the foresight to lay up goods for the future, as well as supply for present needs. This does not allocate for greed. This does not allocate for a thirst of power. We must be mindful of others and see beyond ourselves; for the greater good of the household, community, and rest of the world. Big-picture perspectives are valuable. Be diligent for the sake of your own wellbeing, but there is no virtue in materialism. Hoarding builds no intangible worth. Male and female of humankind might have longer lasting relationships to aid in survival and lifestyle that fits their individuality, laying up goods that could become economically scarce. Always be prepared, but do not hoard greedily. Locke explains that a master of the family could possibly have a wife, children, servants, and slaves, but has no legislative power in the life or death of any of these, and can only claim slaves as property.

Government, according to Locke, has the power to preserve property by the rules it has set up. The right to private property is an inalienable right. We cannot be separated from that which we have earned. People should never be seen as property, and the land and resources we extract and utilize are to be of service in ways that conserve their quality and quantity. We have little established ownership over the land. People and resources are valuable beyond any monetary figure. The use of money creates possibilities for greed which can send us into states of war when we take what we have no right to. These things should be protected by government. Unfortunately paternal law can create biased governments that allow resources to be used in wasteful or specialized ways, in which, a case for reform of the government ought to be called for. On the contrary, having a known and agreed-upon set of rules gives power and peace of mind to those under the power of government. Acquiring property can be a goal, accomplishment, and reward for the innocent who have good work ethic. Nevertheless, protection, slavery, resources, paternal law, and the use of money should be specifically identified by lawmakers. Rules regarding preservation of property were set up and agreed upon by the forefathers of societies and serve the purpose of deciding the differences of interest, whether those differences be civil, violent, victimless, or any other type of criminal offense. The rules deciding differences ought to be a reflection of the soul in comparison with the power of nature (i.e. the will of God). Nature can inspire us to be free spirited and live above the vices of society and the institutions man has created. The laws of society were agreed upon in the past, and we abide by them in the present, and when a man quits a state of nature and enters into civil society, he forfeits the right of punishment over his aggressor to governing officials. Thereby, the citizen turns over judiciary power to the government. "Whenever his property is invaded by the will and order of his monarch, he has not only no appeal [but] he is denied the liberty to be judge of, or defend his right..."

According to Locke, men must give consent to leave the state of nature and enter into political society, and all actions follow the decision of the majority. In a free and peaceful state, the government cannot be forced upon a person even if they are born into the nation of focus, but this is not the way current societies operate. He implies that people can take refuge in the wilderness and remove themselves from both society's luxuries and deficiencies. Paternal society made monarch government appear like a simple solution, an obvious resolution to the threat of injury or invasion. And, the protection of government appeared desirable enough to submit to, and place one's self under, in the variety of its laws and positions.

Competition for resources and differing lifestyles complicated society and created problems that did not exist in a state of nature. Competition *does* exist in a state of nature. In studying the Bible and examining the governments that existed in the time before Christ, the origin of a king, according to Locke, was to lead the nation into battle. After generations of government, subjects who put their trust in a ruler began to feel more misery than safety because of rulers abusing power. Tyranny was explicit when rulers began abusing power. If their use of power was not in the best interest of the people, then explicit use of power could only be used to hurt the people who are supposed to be protected by the very laws that put them in power and the very laws they are now breaking. Among the dangers citizens protect themselves from by placing themselves under government are to the health and safety of a person and the preservation of property. In society, man has the convenience of a settled and known law that whole communities agree upon. In the state of nature, a man has the right to do whatever he sees fit to protect himself and his property and punish any crimes against him by any means he sees reasonable. Unfortunately, in 21st century America, we are not born into a state of nature, nor must we give consent to live under government. All the actions of government ought to be for the common good, or the good of the community. "And all this to be directed to no other end, but the peace, safety, and public good of the people," says Locke.

Whether the government be a democracy, oligarchy, or monarchy, Locke finds them all to be forms of a "commonwealth." By giving up one's rights to the limits of the commonwealth and its legislative power, the legislature can have no more power than the multitude of men supporting the commonwealth. The law governing our own and other men's actions, should be in line with the law of nature i.e. the will of God. We have all been made in the image of the love and strength of God, and for that every person ought to be respected. No one person ought to be diminished nor have more power beyond the multitude of persons supporting the government. Should a man enter into a commonwealth that has extemporaneous directives and/or undetermined resolutions, that man would be in a far *worse* state *in that society* than if he remained in the state of nature. Neither supreme nor legislative power of a commonwealth should be allowed, or have the intention of, taking any man's property, or its goods, without the property owner's consent. This is the purest representation of tyranny; taking away what you have no right to. Tyranny has no place in the world. It undermines the potential goodness that would exist in the world otherwise and creates unnecessary pain and havoc. In any case where one body of government supposes itself to have an opposing interest from the community it serves, taking away what it has no right to, is criminal and unjust. And also, the power of making laws cannot be handed over from one authority to another without the country's people having chosen this transfer of power.

Legislative power doesn't always have business to do, and has no need to always be assembled. Law makers do not need to be in session day in and day out. This raises the question, why is law-making a full-time means of employment? New laws do not need to be made out of boredom. However, execution and enforcement of the law should constantly be active. Locke claims there is a difference between enforcing laws upon citizens of the commonwealth and enforcing laws on those of whom are either foreigners or in the state of nature.

Force without authority puts the government in a state of war unto society if government would be an aggressor. When regulated by true reason, no new legislator needs setup, but rather restores the old and true legislator which was set up for just and fair purposes. And, at that, the world is always in flux, always changing. So, who gets what representation is bound to undergo adjustments. Riches and resources vary over time in respect to where the resources are located, as well as other factors, and as result, the laws regulating them and the lawmakers representing them should not be considered constant. Laws change over time due to their applicability.

For an executive to make decisions on the behalf of his people's best interest where the letter of the law is inapplicable is the executive's "prerogative." Prerogative is nothing more than the power of doing public good without a rule for it. It is doing the right thing, for it is the right thing to do, even when procedural justice is not explicitly defined. Transparency is the key factor in getting the public to believe in good motives. When our true intentions are obvious, the right to make important decisions should be unobstructed. Prerogative appeared largest in the hands of the wisest and best princes of history. Conversely, people would never come together in community, and intentionally put themselves under the rule of those who intended to do them harm. This goes against the nature of rational human beings. Humans have come far through time by using our better judgement. "Reason is the force that unites all of humankind into one fellowship and society."

Three types of power exist in the power spectrum: paternal, political, and despotical. Paternal power being the power parents have over their children, the most limited of the three. Political power being the power governors hold over society for the good of the society, and the preservation of each person's property. Despotical power, the most totalitarian, being a continuation of the state of war and is far removed from reason. Despotical power over-estimates its strength above the laws of God and nature attempting to rule its subjects through fear tactics and aggression. It moves past barriers of morality, attempting to prove something within one's pride and ego. Despots rule by force and fear, taking what it has no right to, demanding respect, of which, none will be given. Political power is also guilty of over-estimating its capabilities, and coercing into effect its own interest. No one, not even princes are exempt from the laws of God and nature, responsible to live in harmony and loving others, accountable for all we do. We are but dust in the wind when compared to the Almighty, and the bonds he holds himself to. God has right to it all, for he made us and everything in the universe. Conversely, a tyrant puts to use power he has no right to. He makes his own will, appetites, and prejudices supersede the law which stands for the good of the commonwealth. A tyrant oppresses with fear. So, may we oppose a tyrannical prince? Should we condemn a tyrant? What about those who are simply irresponsible and take advantage of their position? Just condemnation should come from both God and man, but to act with force can leave the commonwealth in anarchy and confusion. Anarchy might be worth the freedom, although, one sinister regime should not be replaced with another sinister regime. This is often the case when government is dissolved. At what point should a commonwealth dissolve its government? The head of the government and the common class are sometimes judged by a double standard, with the government putting its own interest before the interest of its subjects. But for the head of the government to do unlawful things or make unlawful commands does not excuse the act, just because he is head. Furthermore, it is an abomination of the very authority that put him in power in the first place.

Inroads on a society by a foreigner can cause societies to dissolve, which in turn, would cause its government to dissolve. This is usually carried out by force, creating a state of war whether that be by military force, economic force, or otherwise. Otherwise, the primary cause of the dissolution of government would be from the loss of its own authority within the law-making branches of the government, i.e., lawmakers not following the law. If a ruler's plans show evidence against the liberties of the commonwealth with evil intentions, who is to blame? According to Locke, it is those who put them in their position. This makes the tyrant no less accountable, no more righteous because we now wish to retract our decision to appoint such a person to such a position. The desire to cast off lawful authority, or a ruler's insolence, gives to the rise of disorder. "... whoever, either ruler or subject, by force goes about to invade the rights of either prince or people... is justly to be esteemed the common enemy and pest of mankind."

CHAPTER 17

John Stuart Mill, "On Liberty"

John Stuart Mill was a 19th century English philosopher. In Mill's philosophy book, "On Liberty", Mill detests the idea of tyranny, striking the notion that the public should be free from political tyranny, somewhat as an end in itself, but more so as a means that the world over will reach a richer state through the establishment of liberty. Mill's context of liberty focuses mainly on how it exists in the individual against unjust treatment from the government. He talks about reasons and principles for putting limits on the government. He states government should not exist for self-interest. Government should not be a self-serving body, but rather a limited body governed by the people. Mill states the government has the right to rule and set limits on the individual so that the individual shall not do evil onto others. The idea of accountability of both individuals and the governing body are examined. All should be held accountable, not just those in positions of power.

The heart of the first chapter of the book focuses on the value of individuality, and how it is imperative to nurture the growth of each person. By facilitating growth through the nurturing of free thinking, it is possible to achieve our highest outcome, both as individuals, and a society, in both ability and passion. Spending time in the wilderness nurtures the spirit and facilitates free thinking. Free environments that facilitate liberty are acceptant of opinions and lifestyles which might go against the grain of law, social norms, or both. Mill attacks popular opinions as well as legislation that inhibits natural growth of free thinkers, stating in short that we are holding back the potential of the world by means of political despotism. Granted, many of the freedoms Mill demands have been provided in present day USA. This raises the question, what is classic of political despotism? Running us off of things we have earned and our inalienable rights is despotical. Forcing assimilation is despotical. Coddling us until we become feeble and dependent, and handicapping society is desoptical. Instilling an outlook of overwhelming fear is despotical.

In the second chapter, Mill advocates for freedom of the press to embrace those opinions whose, though unpopular, must be heard. And despite being unpopular these voices still have value for the growth and the enrichment of a nation/community. The church should not muffle the voice of the public. The dogma of the church lays victim to Mill in most of the second chapter, a stifling breath to anyone who goes against the creed of the church. Free thinking sometimes combats Christian tradition. Christian ideology is not focused on stifling innovation. – "Understanding science doesn't make God smaller. It allows us to see divine creative activity in more detail," a quote by Russel Cowburn, a professor of theoretical physics at Cambridge University. - The existence of God does not defuse the mechanics of the universe. Just to the contrary, when you see God working in all things, you become more deeply amazed at the functions of this miraculous universe. Still, Mill was right to the extent that allowing the Catholic church of the middle-ages a hand in making laws diminished the vibrance and enthusiasm of his nation.

Modern American Christianity embraces more of the nuances of the relations people hold with their environment, each other, and their God. Currently, karma and dogma are not seen as quite the opposition they once were. Dogma is doctrine. Karma is action. Positive action should not be hindered by the enslaving doctrine, yet within that doctrine there are traditions and standards for approaching forces of divinity. Tradition and hate are not synonymous. Altruism should be the habit we all adhere to without making too much accommodation for bad behavior. Expectations of forgiveness should not be taken advantage of. Self-righteous convictions based on enslavement to ritual and a lack of love in the heart show no evidence of being a light in the darkness. Facilitating love and nurturing free expression has the capacity to provide goodness to society in ways that approaching God through tradition and ritual might not. The Bible says, "Be quick to listen, slow to speak, and slow to get angry." To Mill, the individual relationship one holds with God is more impactful than etiquette set forth from the church, to the government, and out onto the individuals. He detests the viewpoint of English Christians' of the time toward those outside the church, claiming Christians are condescending and intolerant. The way they carry themselves in public affairs and behind closed doors is nothing to be proud about, as Mill argues. Mill claims we should be released from the bondage of religion in the hope that free thinking will facilitate a more passionate world. Something Mill misses is that our passions must be virtuous to *actually enrich* the world, and that the true aim of tolerance is peaceful communication. Passion and impulse are not *fundamentally* righteous. Nurturing bad behavior does nothing to help those seeking answers. Encouraging individuality for the sake of shock-factor is an abuse of liberty, and has the ability to lead us down wrong paths. If it uses freedom to facilitate the ego towards an end that has no compassion or does not enrich the relationships between people and the world around them, it will surely destroy beautiful harmony. Grooming, excess, and consumption are in no way good uses of liberty. Those are uses of liberty in a self-serving way, purely to the aid of the ego. We ought to find virtuous balance between discipline and liberty.

Aside from Mill's argument, discipline earns respect. Liberty is important but can only be useful when complemented with discipline. Furthermore, discipline is a means of showing respect to other people. Having the discipline to see beyond ourselves and our impulsive desires is the first step towards validating others. It is much the same as being tolerant. The needs of others are seen before the needs of ourselves. We suffer pain and inconvenience for the sake of someone else being comforted. Nature has the ability to teach us respect and discipline. We just have to spend time communing with her. With more respect and discipline, we are freer to act as ourselves *in ways that are valuable to each other*. Predominantly, nature does not record time in nominal fashion. For the individual exercising liberty, nature expresses time in moments of experience. For the world investigating her, nature expresses time in its artifacts, providing evidence of historic environments in the samples the world might collect. Mill flirts with the idea of passion and how passion is facilitated by free thinking. Passion in itself is like money. Without discipline, it leads to bad things. Passion is a means to obtain a greater end. It is neither innocent nor guilty, but the way it is used can render those using it either innocent or guilty. Passion and soul can appear synonymous. Passion for understanding the natural world and spending time with her keeps pure, honest, and innocent souls. Passion for desires of the flesh is bad behavior and bad behavior is easy. It is impulsive and takes no discipline. Navigating nature on the other hand will ask us to react in ways that are far from impulsive, sometimes as an only option of survival. Harmonizing with the flow, and leaning with the momentum can oppose natural reflexes. Keeping a cool head in a high-risk situation requires an element of discipline. Action and reaction condition the soul to navigate the world with discretion and discipline. I believe passion and soul to be synonymous, but I don't believe impulse is a strength. I disagree Mill's statement, "all is lost through the adherence of religious code." Within religious code exist elements of fellowship, prayer, and worship. Humans judging humans is not part of religious code. Praising the Almighty for the grace and power He moves in your life and the lives around you is practicing religion. So is gathering with like-minded people to celebrate the goodness in this life and the goodness promised in the next life. Mill tends to pit theology and morals against each other. When we are indoctrinated to hate those who believe in a relationship with God, we direct ourselves to a doomed fate.

Validly, assuming our own infallibility lies at the heart of Mill's disgust. Being part of a church does not mean you are perfect. Despite serving a compassionate God who offers salvation and inner peace, I don't feel most church goers of present-day America assume their own infallibility. It exists, but on a much smaller scale than it used to. Mill also states that when truth is silenced, even if it is partial truth (as it usually is), then the usefulness of different opinions cannot be explored to discover the rest of the truth. Also, in the loss of silencing the truth is the loss of heartfelt convictions. Heartfelt convictions are often generated from reason and personal experience, and create a more complete scope of truth. Emerson said, "In nature, we return to faith and reason." And, if our reasoning and experience has more variety, the scope of truth will be greater and more accurate. The danger is that the scope of half-lies might be greater as well. We should be careful not to place too much value on personal truths, no matter where they come from. If we find identity through experiences that transcend what is "supposed to be" we should not assume that everyone in our nation and around the world can grasp the significance of the experience. Diverse experiences can build healthier mental well-being, freedom of opinion, and freedom of expression, but we cannot assume universal truth from personal experience. Truth is often found in looking at the same object from many different angles. When the same conclusions are drawn from different perspectives truth is more likely universal and less personal. When we are given the liberty to experience and express things of personal significance, we might enrich the world we live in. We are not called to cancel diversity, no matter if it be traditional or progressive. Mill goes on to talk about individuality as an element of well-being. He expresses the value of diversity and originality, but also acknowledges what experience has taught humankind, knowing that though we are not to copy each other, we can learn from those who have lived before us and build strength in navigating the problems of the world. Knowledge is passed on from generation to generation. Conduct evolves from one generation to the next. We should be careful how we behave because the future of the world depends on it.

Use discretion on what institutions we engage in; as individuals, a nation, a world. When assimilation is requested, even if the assimilation is to become *more* flamboyant, it places a yoke upon us. Putting a yoke upon individuality and breaking the character to obedience weakens the will of man. If we are obedient to evil and not goodness, the world and its future will succumb to evil ambitions. We will be led to pain and destruction. God likes some things we do, and God does not like some of the other things we do. Obedience to God, following the rules, is sometimes tough. Obedience to evil institutions of the world will have us questioning our own character. I disagree with Mill when he says those who act on great impulse are stronger in character. Impulsiveness does not teach us to keep a cool head when situations get a little tricky. It allows for our tempers to cause us to act before we think. That can be a sin and a vice. Every single want and desire that pops through our brains cannot be righteous. Those are our impulses... half-witted desires and fantasies. It offers no moderation. I believe it takes stronger character to control our impulses and act virtuously. Impulse is not always a bad thing. Sometimes our gut reaction can lead us in a good direction, but this relies on how our reflexes are conditioned. What do we pledge allegiance to? Our allegiance will condition our reflexes. I pray our instinctive reflexes are true and righteous.

Mill spends a lot of time talking about the lack of value in Christian morals. The problem is not in what Christian morals are. The problem is superficial Christianity, and how the dogmatic and elite rarely shed real compassion onto those around them. A relationship with God does not require colorless character. Our identity in God can and should be colorful, but with limits and reverence to the Creator of all things. Our conduct and attitude should reflect appreciation for all we have been given. It should be hopeful for a better tomorrow. And we can have individual wants. We should just not behave in ways that push other people away, ways that might steal their hope, or render them inferior. Christian or not, people can be problematic. What Christ taught though is based on two primary commandments: love all people as you would love yourself, and love God, putting Him first above all other things. Some who claim to be Christian behave badly and make others feel inferior. Christians behaving badly does not bring glory to God. Christians making others feel inferior is not a blanket statement, and this particular condition was probably worse in 1800's England where the church and the government were more closely linked. A reasonable question: did the church advise the government, or did the government advise the church? Some people are just looking for a front of being a good person when inside they truly have no faith. Where it gets dicey is when the self-righteous begin making the rules and exploit diverse and original people for the sake of their own advantage. Mill calls us to be individuals, but he also calls us to behave within the rights and interests of others.

Conserving human resources and natural resources helps protect the rights and interests of one another. The value of originality and diversity is to create a more honest scope of customs and cultures, a colorful mosaic of life rooted in universal truth. Colorful and diverse values ought to be protected, but in doing so we cannot cancel universal truth like the right to respect, dignity, and private property. Hopefully, in turn, this creates a stronger mentality and moral code where peace, love, and harmony are sustained. A world in which we can all grow and discover. Existing in a free environment, one without elitist rules and etiquette, is an avenue for creating this richer culture. Still, we should not accommodate stupidity or arrogance whether it be in the name of progress, or tradition. When individual freedom demoralizes the rights of the greater population, individuality does nothing to enrich the culture. Grooming children with alternative sexual lifestyles or church people relentlessly pushing their beliefs on the counterculture, neither directly correlates to goodness.

Mill goes on to talk about the limits on the authority of society. Authority should guide us in the right direction and aim us toward higher pleasures. Wise choices and elevated thinking should be its aim. There are limits to our conduct. But by what virtues do we draw the line? Bizarre is not always best. Sometimes following *tradition* leads to brighter futures. The commodity and use of crystal meth might be vibrant, but I have never heard of it producing positive outcomes. Likewise, a yoke of sexual identity should not be groomed upon our children for a claim to liberty.

Traditions of religion are not demoralizing. Following the conduct of goodness does not rob us of innocence. Moral guidance should be derived from the word of the Almighty, not abstract and obscure suggestions that lack universal truth. Taste and individuality do exist in good ways. Patience and respect lay at the heart of good taste. All of us can continue to be individuals in the presence of God. What is demoralizing within Christianity is putting on an image of goodness while acting in ways that display otherwise. Letting your mouth do more work than your ears is another way of insulting the world around you. Don't push your own ideas upon someone else who has no interest or curiosity about the matter, then punish them when they refuse to accept your ideas. Punishment is God's to mete out, not ours. Mill supported notions of dignity and self-respect, and moved in the right direction when he said our obligations to ourselves and others should not be impeded by extravagance or a short temper. This is what must be balanced in the spectrum: being ourselves yet tolerating every other type of person. Even Jesus said love your enemies and pray for those who persecute you.

It is selfish conduct to *force* others to make sacrifices for us. We should not act in ways that are destructive. Do we all have moral obligation to give guidance and right the wrong? This is an important question to ask ourselves. Grace and forgiveness are a responsibility *from* everyone *towards* everyone. That's a two-way street. No one is more entitled to grace and forgiveness than another. Mills concludes "On Liberty" with applications of individuality and society's limits on free trade, drunkenness, and education. Towards the end of the work, Mill says this, "... a state, which dwarfs its men, in order that they may be more docile instruments in its hands even for beneficial purposes will find that with small men no great [thing] can really be accomplished..."

CHAPTER 18

John Rawls, "A Theory of Justice"

John Rawls was an American Philosopher who published "A Theory of Justice" in 1971. Here I will attempt to summarize his work. Much of this summary is the sentiments of John Rawls and not my own. I included a few of my own opinions, but those are limited. The work seemed very applicable to the civil rights movement, as that was the time in history when it was written and published. Equality, fairness, and equal opportunity ring throughout the text. Rawls work was very long, totaling almost 600 pages in length, so the summary of the work is also long, almost 5,000 words. It gets a little wordy and technical so be prepared. Rawls primary argument is for "justice as fairness" and how equality plays into that. Through justice as fairness, we see a requirement for equal opportunity and equal liberty. Those are achieved by everyone seeing their plan(s) for life through a well-ordered society. And in a well-ordered society, through a bottom-up approach from those least advantaged in society to those most advantaged in society, we all require primary goods to survive and find our place in the world. Distribution of primary goods in a bottom-up approach provides a fairer availability of financial means, economic opportunity, equal representation, available education and training, and realization of self-worth and the value of self-esteem. Distribution of primary goods helps us find peace, liberty, and satisfaction within our social and private lives.

Starting with distribution of benefits, there are greater and lesser shares creating differences within our positions in society. With a greater share of benefits you will likely see more comfort in life. Variable availability of benefits should not be to the disadvantage of any one class of people. Equality helps facilitate fairness and equal distribution of benefits. It is not necessary for every last person to hold an equal amount of benefits, but it is necessary for all people to hold equal representation, opportunity, and liberty. Publicly known and widely understood principles build the groundwork of just systems. Knowledge of the law should be made available to everyone. By these principles we can assign basic rights. By the assignment of these basic rights, we know how to behave. There is also an expectation of cooperation and distribution of burdens. Everyone should pitch in and help carry the load. If we cannot take confidence in the system then suspicion and hostility cause men to act in ways they would otherwise try to avoid. Confidence in the system gives us peace of mind. It gives us hope that we can accomplish almost anything. Variety exists in the quality of living conditions, and living conditions can determine our starting point and our expectations of what a good life is. Living conditions are influenced by different institutions of society that are variable from demographic to demographic. Certain groups of people characteristically have less while others have more. In a system built on justice, the margin between the two ought to be small and less of an obstruction. Institutions like political systems and opportunity of available work can dictate the success of each class of people. Exceptions to the law are expected, but cannot be a topic of focus.

Being impartial in our decisions is a necessary principle. Inclinations of our own good should not affect decisions or principles of a just system. We should not be distorted by our own interests when making decisions for the greater good. As a test, we can presume broad and general presumptions of justice and examine them through the spectrum where they must withstand more specific conditions. Broad and weak presumptions encompass a greater scope of whom these principles can be applied to. With testing, we can revise our presumptions until a more comprehensive theory is developed. Being in flux, Rawls would call it "Reflective Equilibrium," a back-and-forth argument where we can examine the principles for evident proof. "It represents the attempt to accommodate both reasonable philosophical solutions, as well as our considered concept of justice." Dynamics of systems change through time and require adjustments as life moves along.

Injustice is inequalities that are not for the benefit of all, whether they be of egotistic or utilitarian in nature. We should not create inequalities on a basis of prejudice. We should not create inequalities for our own advantage. Still, inequalities are naturally occurring and can exist in just and fair societies. Difference does not directly translate to disadvantage. Differences should not be a mechanism of oppression. Liberties of citizenship and opportunity should be distributed equally. No persons should be denied liberties of dignity and the opportunity to provide for themselves. Rawls reflects a lot on his two principles of justice which are: 1) each person is to have an equal right to the most extensive basic liberty compatible with a similar liberty to others. 2) social and economic inequalities are to be arranged so that they are both reasonably expected to be to everyone's advantage, and attached to positions and offices open to all. This is to be applied in a bottom-up approach to a theory of justice. Those in the lowest classes should be considered first in the application of laws. Lowering the status of the upper class does not directly raise the status of the lower class. This is why a bottom-up approach is most effective. We study the least advantaged to understand the true condition of the whole of society. It sets a baseline of living conditions. When trying to improve the situation of the whole of society, we should concentrate first on the least advantaged. If, primarily, the status of the upper class is lowered, free labor would lower expectation of the lower class. If we cannot place value on *all* classes of people, respect is far too greatly diminished. A person's value extends beyond their usefulness. Unfortunately, from a top-down approach persons are seen as a means to the efficiency of a system. Efficient economies are not necessarily just economies. Just because it produces does not mean it is thoroughly fair. We are still expected to put forth an effort to contribute to the community and cooperate with each other. Defending traditions of freedom is sometimes wrongly influenced by immoral institutions within the system. Institutions that are moral should hold precedent. Institutions that are immoral should be reformed. Though some traditions are, not all traditions are moral. Marriage is one of the greatest examples of a moral tradition. Commitment and responsibility to the health and wellbeing of others is moral.

Rawls advocates equal opportunity of employment and argues that realizing our self-worth comes from work. There is also a necessity for the community that we all must work. There ought to be equal levels of available talent and equal willingness to work. We should realize our self-worth through work and our contribution to the community. Self-worth is not materialistic. We should avoid excessive accumulation of property and wealth, and provide fair opportunities for education, evening out class barriers. "Evening the willingness to make an effort, to try, and so to be deserving in the ordinary sense is itself dependent on happy family and social circumstances." In my opinion, we are all able to try. Rawls claims our willingness to work is dependent on our circumstances. This raises the question, what drives us? A good heart attitude towards God and our communities should drive us to achieve our desires, being that they are moral attitudes and not free-rider (I do me, you follow the rules) or egotistic attitudes. Changing the world starts with the self. I come from a blue-collar, middle-class family. I learned good work ethic from both parents from a young age. I believe good work ethic is important to success. Good work ethic, family, and social circumstances might be dependent on each other, and I admit worse circumstances present more challenges, particularly in one's attitude to achieving success and happiness, but that does not guarantee an outcome. A black friend of mine named

Jonathan Davis once told me, "Hard times make strong people. Strong people make good times. Good times make weak people. Weak people make bad times." And our circumstance should not be a crutch of apathy. Determination is required for everyone, but some will need more of it than others. Determination alone cannot get it done. Somebody somewhere along the line would have to nurture one to fuel success. A strong human should be effective enough to see beyond our circumstance and strive to achieve our goals, but this goes back towards our attitude.

Rawls proposes four positions of justice: 1) System of Natural Liberty 2) Liberal Equality 3) Natural Aristocracy and 4) Democratic Equality. As Rawls classifies them, System of Natural Liberty is open to talents and has a principle of efficiency. Liberal Equality has fair opportunity and a principle of efficiency. Natural Aristocracy is open to talents and exploits differences. Democratic Equality has fair opportunity and embraces and utilizes differences. Democratic Equality is his most favored position which he claims as the original position for his argument.

When differences are embraced *and* there is equal opportunity, it is easier to realize our self-worth. We can be who we are and make a contribution. We cannot all be the most advantaged; this is just not realistically possible. Wealth and talent are not in direct relation to each other, no matter how much society wants you to believe that. Some people have more money than they do heart, soul, mind, or strength. Having a passion for something does not mean you could or should get rich doing it. But that does not mean the world won't be a better place because of the talent God has given you. Should you be able to acquire primary goods for those same efforts? Yes, that would be fair, but dignity and deep self-expression do not require fat bank accounts. We all have something unique to offer the world, and we are not all the same. Differences and diversity are naturally occurring, and should be embraced, not exploited or made null and void. Overcoming challenges builds character. Pitting ourselves against each other because of our differences solves nothing. We must embrace who we are and create opportunities, especially for those least advantaged. By offering opportunity and embracing equal citizenship, our self-worth is realized by intangible factors like personal nature and our contributions to the community. High status is not valuable in defining high self-worth. Positions are justified only when those better off succeed in the same system where the least advantaged succeed. When those with the most expect more, it robs those who have who have lesser primary goods and self-worth. Funny how the wealthy expecting to get wealthier hurts the lower class the most... a rather tyrannical scheme. No social or economic scheme can replace the value of each of us acting virtuously and respectfully to all people. If we hold the lower class out of offices and positions that the higher class holds, we are not only excluding them from economic opportunity, but also the realization of self-worth that comes from exercising social duty.

Distributing shares of equality (primary goods, opportunity to work and make decisions, self-worth) is a matter of procedural justice, perfect procedural justice. The person doing the distributing should be the most impartial in their decisions. They must have no more to gain out of unequal distribution than of equal distribution. "Suppose the law and government act effectively to keep markets competitive, fully employed, and property and wealth widely distributed by the appropriate forms of taxation, or whatever, to guarantee a reasonable social minimum. Assume also there is fair equality of opportunity underwritten by education for all; and that the other equal liberties are secured... In this complex of institutions, which we think of establishing social justice, in the modern state, the advantages of the better situated improve the condition of the least favored... setting the social minimum at an appropriate level." This is an example Rawls presents where inequalities are to the advantage of all people. It appears a little contradictory to his bottom-up approach to justice as fairness, but still a valuable thought. If the upper class has more resources to provide for the needs of the lower class there is greater possibility to improve the situation of the least advantaged. We must judge the health of an economy by the conditions of the least advantaged. Complete fulfillment of everyone's desire has no moral consideration. Complete fulfillment of everyone's desires is biased and imperfect because we are acting based on our own advantage. Also, providing for every last one of our wants does not nurture character such that we can express our nature and plans for life for the benefit of social unions.

Perfect procedural justice accommodates for changing positions and removes the deciding individual from needing to have character because the procedure itself provides justice as fairness instead of the decision maker requiring justice. Perfect procedural justice also accounts for the changes and dynamics as people and resources cycle about. This is where "reflective equilibrium" comes into play. Rawls raises the question of how expectations are supposed to be estimated. This estimation questions what primary goods are necessary in all different walks of life to live out our purposes. Just as our means and our needs are not always in healthy proportion, there are issues of variable distribution, rational prudence, and a goal of fair equality of opportunity. Opportunity to provide for ourselves and make contributions to the community are considered primary goods as well. Occupational positions as civil service agents provide an opportunity to give back to the community, express our nature, and provide an income for ourselves. These things help carry out our plans for life, realize our nature, and live for the benefit of social unions. But they must be done in a spirit of honesty and fairness.

Principles of justice, laws, assume there are not multiple meanings of good, and that we all understand this. The law should be well defined, understood by all, and be applied in a method of equal citizenship and equal opportunity. We should not have to question the definition of the law. The law as it is defined should be equally applied to all people. A biblical idea of "good" can be pulled from its definition of Fruits of the Spirit which are love, joy, peace, kindness, goodness, faithfulness, gentleness, and self-control. So, where must we source our definition of good, and how can this definition be publicly known? When it comes to questions of wealth, acquiring more can only work into a theory of justice if it improves the situation of those who have less. Biblically though, charity is not the responsibility of the government. That is the responsibility of individuals with the willingness to give. If government creates a fair distribution of primary goods, what would this look like? Positions of civil service provide individuals a means of earning a living, providing for themselves, and making contributions to the community. It is an opportunity that should be available to all. There is a minimum needed to make contributions to the community, and carry out our plans for life, but an excess is not necessary. We often assume that more is better or necessary when that is not truly the case. Still, we assume that everyone prefers more. We must have the temperance to not always desire more. We need to give it a break and rest from the drive to achieve and acquire more. Sometimes those who desire less are happier than those who have an excess.

More equality and more fairness are intangible, not material wealth. Equal citizenship is something we should strive to acquire in a just system. Equal citizenship supports justice as fairness and is something society is still trying to achieve. Equal citizenship levels the playing field and allows for diverse occupation of positions in society. Equal citizenship allows all classes of people to make important decisions. Social positions appear to Rawls as a better indicator of social and economic inequalities than wealth and income. "...justice as fairness appraises the social system from the position of equal citizenship and the various levels of income and wealth." No matter our background, all moral persons should have the opportunity to make important decisions. The assignment of basic rights based on sex and race are almost never to the advantage of the least favored. Redress to provide the disenfranchised with better opportunities should be the responsibility of society, namely providing better education so the disenfranchised can take part in the affairs of society and secure a sense of self-worth. "In justice as fairness men agree to share in one another's fate... natural distribution of talents and endowments is neither just nor unjust...what is unjust is the way institutions of society choose to deal with these differences."

Rawls explores the idea of fraternity as an element within his theory, and does so in a slightly augmented use of its usual meaning. He states that fraternity is a case where we include each other and do not wish to gain without others within the fraternity gaining also. This is most common in the case of family. Here fraternity has an inclusive meaning and not an exclusive one. How does fraternity relate to fellowship, which is 'friendly association, especially with people who share one's interests'? Fellowship is a biblical obligation and expectation of Christian believers as their faith matures. Fellowship is mostly an action, spending quality time together, celebrating together, and guiding one another by shared beliefs. Rawls' use of fraternity is very similar to fellowship. Looking out for others and not only ourselves is important, but this warrants sacrifice. We should show temperance in our wants. The mere existence of other humans prevents us from obtaining every one of our impulsive desires. We are taught the value of sharing from a young age for a reason. Social dynamics require us to maintain a balance with other people. The idea of competition comes to light, but even that should be cooperative and not greedy. Competition can be prudent and altruistic. All others acting justly so we get our own demands is egoism. This is an example of "free-rider" perspective where "I do me, you follow the rules." Our own demands are not of the gretest interest to the community. It is the destruction of beauty for the sake of the ego. We are called not to be greedy, looking out for only our own interests, but instead only wish to gain if the others around us gain as well. Rawls claims the way we behave depends on our circumstances. That I disagree with. We are all expected to have self-control. We are called to see beyond ourselves and our circumstances; to have an attitude of hope and perseverance.

According to Rawls, equilibrium is reached in free market economies when players and traders freely give to the taste and obstacles of others. Cooperation within the community is beneficial to the individual. Ideally, competition would be relatively equal and resources moderately available. Though competition is real, if its aims and interests are based in sentiment and affection, then those aims are in the interest of advancing the wellbeing of others. Conversely, if our aims are towards wealth, position, influence, and the accolades of social prestige, then they are in the interest of the ego and do nothing to improve the wellbeing of others, but rather destroy harmony.

Much of Rawls' argument rests on a principle he defines as a "veil of ignorance." The "veil of ignorance" is basically a hypothetical mechanism of just society where we do not make decisions in favor of our own interests or to the opposition of those we are in competition with. Particulars of a "veil of ignorance" are that we know very little about our own circumstances, or that of our opposition, while both parties make decisions in favor of systems working toward justice and equality. These decisions should not be happened upon by inclinations of our own advantage. The concept of right should be general, not exactly universal. They should be in accordance with God's will. They should have virtues of morality. They should be publicly known and support social cooperation. Force, and threat-advantage are not to be used in developing a concept of justice.

This system of principles is to be final. The ruling of disputes should not be appealed just because we do not like the outcome. This system of principles rules out egoism, dictatorship, and free-rider (I do me, you follow the rules) principles of justice.

Altruism and disinterestedness should be the principle-rationale in developing a theory of justice. Pointless and arbitrary principles should be neglected. Nuanced laws often oppress particular classes of people.

Racial and sexual discrimination are not only unjust, but also irrational. They are only means of suppression.

Sometimes when we make decisions, we don't really have good options to choose from. We are forced to choose the least of the evils. When choosing the least of evils we should be skeptical of calculated probabilities. We should not get lost in the numbers or place too much trust in models. It is good to look to a decisionmaker who cares very little about their own circumstances. Instead, look to see they have a concept of good, rejecting outcomes that hardly anyone can accept.

Improving the condition of those better off will hopefully cause them to invest in the training and encouragement of the available working class. Stock of available working class depends on those who are willing, available, and capable to work. We cannot pool resources that do not already exist. If there is no one willing to work, then there will be no working class to operate the necessary positions within the economy. If we choose to put forth no effort, those who *are* willing to work will take all the authority to make decisions for us. Competitive economics with an open class system where there is socio-economic mobility cannot accommodate for *excessive* inequalities. Excessive inequalities are to the disadvantage of everyone within these social unions. Those who are marginally poor have a harder time making even initial improvements than those who do not live in such a state of scarcity. The greater the margin between the rich and the poor greater inequality, and as a result, both the upper class and the lower class suffer. Competitive economics rely on the motivation to improve our own condition, too. We must be willing to make the sacrifices needed to achieve more. Still, this does not mean that in a just society we are given all we want. We must make a diligent effort and earn the things we desire.

Rawls discounts utilitarian concepts of justice, stating a small portion of the population suffering for the greater good is unreasonable. To take from the unwilling, or to spend money that is not yours is not an action of justice. Rawls detests utilitarian concepts as they make assumptions about having the means to make good ends. Utilitarianism asks us to make sacrifices for the greater good, but if we have less to offer it can be demoralizing to give up what little we have to improve the conditions of most others.

We prefer to exist in social settings that offer the highest prospects. More available resources create the possibility for a higher quality of life. There should still be a distinction between material and intangible qualities that enrich life. A proper theory of justice should protect basic rights and ensure against worst eventualities. Safety and prosperity are principles of justice. In a fair and just system, the health and well-being of every individual in the community should be our focus. Having a reasonable source of primary goods and distribution of those by publicly known law in an effort to sustain health and prosperity is a function of a just system. The challenge is keeping the agreements you make in good faith, agreements that are open knowledge to the public, and agreements within the limits of our morality and responsibility. A system of justice is stable when everyone is interested in buying into the program. It must accommodate all classes. The hope is that it might fulfill everyone's needs. Wants and desires have secondary priority to our needs. *Expecting* participation in a theory of justice does not automatically fulfill needs, wants, and desires. Still, everyone is required to *participate* knowing they cannot have everything they want, but at the same time understanding the good of the self and the good of society are dependent on everyone making contributions. A *request* of sacrifice and participation is not engagement in social function(s). It takes compliance to procedure to engage in social function(s). It takes real contributions from every class of people to engage in the social function of a just system. No one's livelihood should be diminished to accomplish just society.

Self-respect ought to be the biggest driving force of us buying into a theory of justice. Value and worth drive us to make good decisions. Self-respect is both a cause and effect of how we respect others. If we respect ourselves, we are more likely to respect others. If we respect others, we are more likely to respect ourselves. These two scenarios might not happen simultaneously but do coincide with each other. Having an element of respect living within your soul will be expressed to all people should it actually exist within you. Something that differs between people are what qualifies us for deserving respect. Personally, honesty and fairness qualify respect. For a system to be just, the vast majority of people must agree on the set of values that deserve respect. Rawls gets into defining 'good people' later. Goodness deserves respect. Should respect exist within you, it will be expressed both toward yourself and toward others. It aids in the function of well ordered society as we cooperate to accomplish shared objectives, and show sensitivity to the needs of everyone within society. We ought to respect the rights of people, thoroughfare. Sometimes grace and dignity need to be explicitly stated in writing for our leaders to acknowledge these things in a spirit of equality.

Impartiality, mutual disinterestedness, and self-respect are greater driving forces of just society than sympathy. Sympathy, according to Rawls, is a weak driving force of justice as fairness. Rawls wants to see people doing the right thing for the sake of doing the right thing, not virtue signaling. If love were the primary driving force of justice as fairness, how would justice be executed? Love alone gets scrambled when the claims of several persons conflict. Love preserves each person. Love disciplines. Love shows discernment. And love never discriminates. Love gives everyone equal representation as moral beings, and as Rawls admits, is more comprehensive than justice as fairness, yet more complex. Justice as love is more likely to make right decisions in place of the law where there is no law. It is often said "God is love."

Moral and religious obligations are self-imposed as Rawls claims. They do not exist naturally within us as to say they are not instinctive. Moral and religious obligations should not persecute or oppress equal liberty for all persons. We should not forcefully push our beliefs no matter which end of the tradition-progress spectrum we sit upon. Equal liberty does not allow for a free-for-all. It simply means we all operate under the same limits, although all persons deserve to enjoy the full scope of liberties within these limits.

Rawls looks to Mill's argument that institutions that give greater opportunity for experience build richer societies that are more passionate and vigorous. We shall give opportunity for experience, but at what point should we set limits, and at what degree of morality should these limits exist? We all have to adhere to the same limits. We must cooperate to achieve harmony. We must work together to achieve both our own plans for life and the plans of the community or society, all with equal citizenship. The state can favor no particular religion. Some religions embrace altruism, but I do not know of one that is based on fairness. "The government has no authority to render associations either legitimate or illegitimate any more than it has the [same] authority in regard to art or science." Moral and spiritual interests should be regulated to align with equality. Limiting the power for moral and spiritual groups should be done to offer equal opportunity. Liberty should be limited in the name of public order and security. The good of society should be acknowledged in deciding our limits, but still allow for experience and expression of our own nature. It's a fine line to walk.

Equal liberty must be granted in moral and religious pursuits, as those make up a person's identity and helps them express their nature. We must tolerate those we do not agree with (this statement going as far back as Jesus saying to "love your enemies"). The true objective of tolerance is that we, with all our different views, will communicate peacefully. Toleration supports the fact that specialized ideology is not justified in the greater system, that is, the general public cannot comprehend specialized ideology, so it mustn't be the mode of operation. "While an intolerant sect does not itself have the title to complain of intolerance, its freedoms should not be restricted [except] when the tolerant sincerely and with reason believe that their own security and that of the institutions of liberty are in danger... The just should be guided by the principles of justice and not by the fact the unjust cannot complain." To what degree do we attribute the goodness of the supernatural? Are we amazed with fear and wonder at God? And are we respectful to all people for we have all been made in the image of the love and strength of God? When a façade of freedom cries at restrictions, those cries need to be examined for truth, universal truth. We need to offer guidance and not shame. Just as we tolerate the dispositions of those we disagree with, we cannot cry wolf when the opposition sets restrictions that align with universal truth and the greater good. Our rights and liberties need to be made not only in the name of experience but also in the name of discipline, such that we can cooperate to carry out the functions of well-ordered society. If these functions do not align with the expression of our own nature, you may have the right to complain, but not the right to label who the dangerous people are. This section approached the idea of equal liberty and tolerating the intolerant, not asking for yourself what you are denying from others. Complaining over petty problems does not describe a tolerant people. Tolerant people hold their tongue over the urge to give impulsive rebuttal. We have the duty to act in the best interest of our society and the generations that will inherit it.

Rawls poses the question 'what defines a good person?' Performing well in our various roles? Bettering society? Rawls claims broadley based properties, not specialized ones, defines good people. Properties such as the *strong effective desire to act on the basic principles of right* are broad enough to give the groundwork for defining good people as well as things like *wanting others to have basic virtues, if one's plan for life follows the conditions of right and goodness* and *wanting others to acknowledge these same restrictions and conditions.* In a specialized sense, a person can have greater quality with attributes like intelligence, imagination, strength, endurance, and cooperation, providing they are not an evil genius. Taking action to advance the good of other persons are also qualities of a good person. Conversely, bad men thirst for power and authority to control and manipulate others. Evil men harbor love for injustice.

Self-respect is a primary good, and justice as fairness accommodates self-respect. It is a matter of how we value ourselves. Self-respect gives us confidence in our interests, endeavors, and plans for life. Not being tricked and appreciating the grace and talents we make available to the world allows us to build self-respect. Those can give us a rough approximation of how much we respect ourselves. Plans for life, endeavors, and interests are validated by our accomplishments and the people we surround ourselves with. People who have common interests in the same goals we ourselves hold can offer us validation. All of this gives us a sense of what we are doing is worthwhile. As a society, it is important for us to support and make available organizations, associations, and communities where people feel validated and realize self-respect. Through self-respect we express our nature in moral ways in a spirit of fairness. Shame and regret are the antithesis to self-respect. It is unnecessary for us to feel ashamed because of our abilities or appearance. There can be absolutely no shame in doing the best with what God has given you. Regret from failure to live out our plans for life and from behavior of betrayal make us feel unworthy and rob us of self-esteem. Accepting the things we cannot change and behaving honestly build self-esteem and good social unions.

A major condition for equal justice is the capacity for moral personality. This exists in almost all of us. There is no whole race or recognized group of humans that lack the capacity for moral personality. Justice as fairness is not a tool of maximizing liberty but rather equality. A person who has the potential, though possibly not yet developed, should also have their equality protected. A capacity for justice ensures everyone has equal rights. There is no prerequisite to treat people with equality, fairness, and respect, as that is in the nature of justice.

Goodness, self-respect, and moral capacity facilitate equality and justice as fairness. Those three qualities should be strived for. Moral convictions must not be a result of coercive indoctrination. They must be developed within the individual through experience and the guidance of wise friends. We have the autonomy and objectivity to judge for ourselves. Goodness, self-respect, and moral capacity should be strived for. Hopefully we are all born with good sense and use our better judgement in the decisions we make. Instruction aids in understanding, but we must be prudent in who we allow to instruct us. Our concept of justice should not be *primarily* influenced by tradition or authority. As Timothy Leary put it, "Question authority, and think for yourselves." There will always be a spectrum of what we define as goodness but hopefully it is not too polarized that just society becomes an impractical expectation. Basing our definition of goodness in universal truth gives us faith, confidence, and admiration toward achieving goodness. Society has to constantly pursue equilibrium and righteousness and commit in good faith to agreements that equally represent all persons. "In time of social doubt and loss of faith in long established values, there is a tendency to fall back on the virtues of integrity: truthfulness, sincerity, lucidity, and commitment, or as some say, authenticity... A tyrant might also display these attributes to a high degree and by doing so exhibit a certain charm..." We must be prudent in who we trust and what we believe.

Acting on the basic principles of right, virtue, and goodness, and wanting to see the same from the world around us shows quality in character. It allows us to build self-respect. Wise choices and improving the world facilitate these things. Experience can help us develop good judgement, and discipline will allow us to adhere to it. We all have the moral capacity to treat people fairly. Everyone's rights should be protected, and we should always strive for equality. These convictions ought to dwell within us and not be the result of coercive indoctrination. With experience and the guidance of wise peers we can put a theory of justice into practice.

Does well-ordered society achieve the good of a community? Does it offer equal opportunity and equal liberty in ways that allow us to express our nature in a fair way, making contributions to the social union bettering not only our own lives but also the lives around us? Well-ordered society gives us confidence in the availability of primary goods and also sustaining health and comfort. Though well-ordered society is a cooperative venture for mutual advantage, society is often in a conflict of interests because of competition. Competition can earn self-worth but can also create disadvantages for those who try but do not succeed. How do we resolve this conflict where some succeed and some do not? Conflict can be dissolved where principles of society are most general, principles that build common ground between those who succeed and those who do not. If our principles are general, then finding common ground between conflicting interests is more obtainable. In finding common ground, we should humble ourselves, show self-discipline, and see beyond ourselves. Principles which are broad and open to all have a greater propensity of achieving a greater common goal. Broad and open principles are also the types of principles used to define a good person. We cannot be too specialized in our criteria for defining good people. If our principles are to move with fairness, opposing interests can still move with cooperation to achieve a collective goal. Social order of private society can be organized that the collective people are either competing or independent, but all complementary of each other. Rawls states institutions of society can be seen as a means to our private aims. In this, most of us prefer schemes that give each person the largest possible share of assets. Division of advantages is controlled by balance of power, yet must be fair and mutual. Stability of just and efficient arrangements requires the use of sanctions. Unfortunately, we cannot all get what we want, the way we want it, all the time. There must be restrictions to find balance in both fairness and efficiency.

It is sometime contended that private society is ideal when there is a suitable standard of reciprocity. Give and take are equal. Social nature of humankind contrasts the concept of private society. Though competing, we must work in concert with one another. We need partners and we need to engage in activities for the sake of the activity, for the necessity and compliment of our own good. Orderly pursuit of our interests depends on complementary capacities and appreciation of others. We are to enjoy one another and recognize the good of each other's part in the whole of society, especially as they assist in our own plans for life. Cultural contributions will overlap, and we must appreciate others. Histories will overlap and we must collectively pursue them further, solving the problems of the past and prudently following our paths into the future. My own thought: we must reflect on the actions taken in the past to remedy problems and be honest as we progress into the future about the accomplishments that have been made, giving as much credit as we can to those who pioneered such success.

Dr. Martin Luther King Jr. and his associates did accomplish a good measure of progress. If the improvements from the 1960's through the 2020's are ignored, denied, or neglected, you are also denying the efforts and achievements of every civil rights activist in history. Also, climate and environment has progressed from the time before environmental policy until now, and this goes back much further than just air quality policy. To deny this progress is to deny the hard work and innovation of every environmental scientist and field worker in history. Quitting progress is not what I'm proposing, but appreciating the progress that has been made; reflecting, and re-evaluating our approach into the future is necessary. We must maybe even endure the lag time between initiating change and seeing the effects to understand the real results of our actions.

We must interpret social tradition. In this we find our connections, and in social union we must connect with elements of affection and friendship... work toward the greater good... a collective achievement requiring cooperation from all. Still, our similar wants can put us at odds, competition. Society aims at complementary relationships. Society is the collective function of all people, and we must function with conduct that is for the good of everyone, despite competing interests. The mosaic of competing interests creates a diversified culture. Art and science, religion and culture contribute to this. They are dynamic values that express individual nature and enrich the color of the community. Even those separated widely by history and circumstances have the ability to cooperate in realizing their common nature. "...members of a well-ordered society have the common aim of cooperating together to realize their own and another's nature in ways allowed by the principles of justice." When we encourage each other, and each succeeds, we realize our nature as moral beings, independently and collectively. Encouragement and guidance are valuable in realizing our nature as moral beings. Over time and generations, the development of society can enrich our plans for life. The values held by generation after generation build a belief system on which just society can exist, and we can all prosper.

Obedience and order, though suffering the pains of discipline, help us express our own nature in ways that improve the condition of the society. When society is in a downward spiral we should look to the past and identify when and why things started going wrong and attempt to correct our direction. This is also a means to the realization of justice. Affirming just institutions takes appreciation and enjoyment in one another through cooperation. "The public realization of justice is a value of community."

Even in the workforce, we should strive to contribute to societies that obtain elements of suitable expression and are less burdensome. We should pursue work that nurtures our own nature and helps stabilize just institutions of society. Still, we are dependent on each other for many reasons. We rely on each other. Everything we have comes from somewhere else. Each one of us should make an effort to facilitate the good of society, to make society function better for the intrinsic needs of each one of us. Once a certain standard of living conditions are met, liberty holds priority and we no longer desire material things to enrich our lives. Spiritual and cultural pursuits become obtainable and more valuable, and material wants hold less urgency. Increasing the productivity and economic efficiency beyond a certain limit due to excessive material wants pushes society into a state of where no one will ever be satisfied and renders a greater burden on the resources we have available. When material wealth blocks opportunity for soulfulness, justice is not alive. Changes need to be made. Equal rights and equal liberty can accommodate for this lack of soulfulness. It is not productivity and efficiency that must be maintained, at least not in an economic sense. It is connecting with reality. Status based on material wealth does nothing for the soulfulness of the world. Richness in the soul is brought about by the opportunity for experience and the availability of primary goods; self-esteem and equal opportunity.

In a theory of self-unity, Rawls detests hedonism and its aims of pleasurable experiences as the ultimate end, arguing justice as fairness holds a higher standard based on moral personalities versus capacity for pleasure. Plans for life are seen as a primary goal in justice with equal representation for all persons. Right and good have definitive limits. When the principle of a well-ordered system is justice, we can live out our plans within these limits, and our own plans for life support the greater good of society.

In conclusion, a sense of justice which is thorough hinges on well-ordered society where all individuals authentically pursue justice in each of their own lives. There must be equal opportunity, equal liberty, and equal citizenship. We should realize our own moral plans for life and work in cooperation to achieve this. In doing this we develop self-esteem and self-worth. We must all be accountable to the community, bound by ties of affection and fellow feeling. We must be honest and feel the impact of our actions, both good and bad, in a wide-reaching sense. We humans have a desire to express our nature, and as moral persons, a just society would assist this. If a well-ordered society that hinges on honesty and fairness does not work for you... "It is, of course, true that in their case just arrangements do not fully answer to their nature, and therefore, other things equal, they will be less happy than they would be if they could confirm their sense of justice. But here one can only say: their nature is their misfortune" – John Rawls.

CHAPTER 19

William J. Federer, "Socialism: The Real History from Plato to the Present"

William J. Federer wrote the book, "Socialism: The Real History from Plato to Present" contesting the efficiency and fairness of socialism and communism. The heart of the argument was that socialism is a pretense to communism, and in both, less liberty exists. Inalienable rights are taken from the citizens in an effort to make them subservient to the state, and the state never fully provides the treasures it promised at the beginning. Federer presents many historical facts about the communist movement and how that has almost always been spawned from socialism. The socialist movement finds origins in Ancient Greece and the Roman Empire through the Middle Ages and the French Revolution, Nazi Germany, Russia and the Soviet Union, Southeast Asia, and the United States of America. Hundreds of social and political quotes are listed to support Federer's argument in an apparently honest and patriotic fashion. I wanted to include this piece to clarify many of the claims about the socialist movement in America, and how it parallels many of the tyrannical powers we face today, hopefully to educate younger generations on the perils that come with socialist ideology. Socialism never seemed to provide the utopia it chased, yet much of Millennial and Gen Z generations handsomely eye the treasures socialist bureaucrats advertise. Where socialism has worked in the favor of the people there is always one key factor: a universal willingness to work.

Socialism and communism preach equality and abundance that it cannot produce. It preaches a larger-than-life lifestyle available to all people. It speaks to our desires to live lavishly. The reality is, no matter how you manipulate the system, there is no possible way to provide luxury to all people. The simple fact of scarcity of resources makes such a position impossible. Limited availability of goods will always demand competition, or, at the least, rationing of what is available. This creates a spectrum of wealth spanning from poor to rich in which we are all forced to live. There is and always will be variability in the social scope. Material needs do not create richer and happier lives, but the desire to acquire more of those things always speaks to our impulsive desires and causes us to want systems that can do just that. A spectrum of material wealth is not inherently problematic. We are called by God to be content in all situations. What is problematic is how our desires are weaponized against us to usher in totalitarian authority that runs the deep-state contributing nothing but fear, coercion, and oppression over the people they were supposed to liberate.

In a socialist nation, the people are not in control. Liberties are diminished and decided upon by government leaders. The institutions of society, marriage, religion, the workforce, private property, and the means of recreation, are re-created in a godless image. They convey lack of morality that stems from the lack of God in society and the denial of God's eternal truths. Inalienable rights do not exist. Respect is diminished and fear is generated. Communism and socialism are self-serving and only fulfill the power-thirst for the deep-state, not actually providing what it advertises: a country that does not need a workforce / excessive material wealth. For the working-class, self-worth, private property, and a sense of accomplishment, are held ransom by the state. Primary goods are rationed by the state. Extreme rates of inflation are excused by the reformation in the name of liberty that they are leading. In no way can these features aid in the quality of life for the working class and the impoverished.

The ones the socialist government was supposed to help the most it belittles the most. Instead, the money goes to bureaucrats and the affluent. To them, all that is important is control and authority. Once given power, the thirst for power multiplies and can never be fully satisfied. As a result, those under the reign of the government (which we all inescapably are) exist under the will and opinion of the ruling class. To communist and socialist rulers there is *nothing more than what we see in this world*. They preach worldly extravagance when in reality we should all be able to find satisfaction with common and ordinary lives; lives that are good, free, and with due justice. Socialism preaches to our desires with hollow doctrine that exploit the impulsiveness of human nature. They are exploiting our differences and make us view our differences as problems, creating tension that is not necessary. Progress should always be worked towards, but *real solutions* do not come from an augmented view of the actual problem. It's hard to make progress without hard work. People should not be brainwashed that we are inherently enemies of each other. We were all made in the image of the love and strength of God, and for that, we all deserve respect and equality. We should not embrace evil when unsettled people attempt to destroy good unions within communities and society. Attempts to destabilize and divide us need to be seen for what they are: devices to put most of the power in the hands of a few. Self-respect should not be sacrificed in the name of the movement. And no matter how plain and traditional it appears, a relationship with God gives us worth and identity. It shows us our calling, giving us a sense of purpose, strength, and a sense of accomplishment; things socialism and communism will try to take away.

Our desires make us vulnerable. Being a unique individual and having an identity *can be had* without fulfilling *all* of our impulsive desires. A relationship with God gives us identity and satisfaction in good and ordinary ways, and we don't have to cling to the things that make us feel flamboyant or extreme to feel loved and happy. It is human nature to feel that we need to impress others or earn our value to be happy and have identity. It is also human nature to doubt things, but also human nature to see horizons. Horizons should be approached with curiosity in discovering truth, to put forth faith instead of doubt. That is the means available to all people at no cost that can make us feel loved, happy, and give us identity. Feeling loved as the individuals we are with specific needs and desires shouldn't rely on the institutions of society to facilitate that love. God really loves us. Self-worth is attained through virtue. We build character by perseverance. Greed and power are *not* God-given avenues towards self-worth, although greed and power are the driving forces of the deep state. Wealth and power exist unharnessed when we try to put divine authority in the hands of man. Many don't like to hear it but prayer, worship, communion (with sacraments and creation), and obedience are methods of developing a relationship with God that gives us self-worth. The love of God is real if you search for it.

Fulfillment-of-desires by socialist doctrine will not create a just society. With the deep-state, fairness and honesty are ignored in the pursuit of power. In socialist society desires are rarely fulfilled, and justice is often trampled on. True liberty and justice are what God expects out of us. Equal opportunity, the will to work, and expressing our nature in ways that are beneficial to well-ordered society are features aligned with the will of God. If the press is controlled by a godless deep-state, there is no freedom. The narrative is controlled by those in power, and unless the masses see beyond the lies, they will never take the power back. The media has the ability to mold our concept of right and wrong if Biblical truth is removed from our concept of right and wrong. The word of God is steadfast and omniscient. It sets limits that are ignored by a media speaking to the desires of the people. Most who pursue the Bible's teachings find the wisdom they were seeking, and are able to use it to live successful lives. When we remove these truths from the narrative of society, the propensity for lies to mold our lifestyles becomes dangerously overwhelming. If the media is used to sensationalize our problems, they will promote division amongst us and socialism will conquer all people, uniformly. When the ruling elite establishes what comes through the media, they control the opinions of everyone who tunes in. Virtue is replaced by trends and popularity. Whoever is trendy and followed has the ability to dictate the narrative. Whatever opposes their opinion is shamed or canceled. In this way, their opinion is the only opinion that matters.

Creating disturbances creates the need for aid, causing dependency. Destabilizing well-ordered society creates crises that persuade the people to give up freedom to politicians who establish a new status quo. People who have been destabilized and unsettled find themselves cornered and offer their submission to the most generous hand willing to help them out of whatever mess they're in. In this way, the crisis destabilizes our lifestyles to a point that we all become hostile and even more impulsive. Hostility only creates irrational decision making. We must ignore those who entice hostility for the cause of establishing their own humanly, imperfect standard upon their individually, limited viewpoint. "Crisis incidents are manufactured to cause groups to attack each other... people panic in fear and easily surrender their freedoms to any politician who promises to restore order and security." Federer quoted attorney general William Barr, "The tacit goal of this project is to convert all of us into 25-year olds living in the government's basement, focusing our energies on obtaining a larger allowance rather than getting a job and moving out." Polarizing the people creates tension so all that has to be done for revolution is to manufacture a crisis if the luck to have a real one doesn't already exist.

Trying to develop heaven on earth is a futile endeavor. We must endure the trials of earth faithfully and obediently to enjoy the real treasure of the true heaven. Here we can only produce imperfect replications. When leaders with egotistical agendas try to develop a perfect world, their world their way, the citizens become slaves to the state, devalued and disposable. Consolidating control benefits no one. Socialism and communism are a beautiful dream in the thought phase then turn to a nightmare once it's established. It's not about helping the poor. It's about power. The elite ruling class will advertise free, free, free, then remove your liberties and decision-making ability under the ideology that they are smarter than you. This is done such that they gain the position that allows them to make all decisions about how you and I go about our lives. It's power for the sake of power. These are big government solutions to real world problems, but instead of providing real solutions they only build a government big enough that can take away everything we have.

Rewriting history so we devalue our heritage softens our values and allows our minds to be reconditioned to embrace the new narrative. Brainwashing is regular practice in strict communist countries where values are soften then, usually by force, those who contradict the state are traumatized, then rehabilitated with stately ideology to have a disposition of obedience and subversion to the forces of the autocratic society.

Federer approaches the ideas of charity and property, outlining from a biblical standpoint who is responsible to take care of the sick and the poor. The church and individuals who willfully give should help those they can. It is not the government's responsibility to alleviate poverty. Any money the government has is not its own. It is not charity to give away something that is not yours. Furthermore, the usurpation of property robs dignity from those who earned it. Property cannot be taken by the government and redistributed evenly across the population to alleviate poverty.

Federer states that at the inception of the US Constitution, government of the people, by the people, for the people was unprecedented. Not even in the city states of Ancient Greece did the citizens have such autonomy over their government. And by opposing the symbols (like the flag, the constitution, and the national anthem) of this great nation one also opposes the autonomy by which the people rule themselves. Up until this point in time, people have only been ruled by kings and dictators of sorts. The closest reflection to what exists in America was the Jew's covenant with God in ancient Israel, where the people had equal citizenship and were obedient to God who ruled from above. Federer cites Calvin Coolidge saying, "They (colonial clergy) preached equality because they believed in the fatherhood of God and the brotherhood of man." The biggest challenge is to resist the urge to be selfish. Corrupted morals propose a threat to perpetuating freedom. No conservative government can sustain without the gospel. No liberal government can sustain without sound conduct. "When one realizes God loves them, it helps them to love others", said Federer.

CHAPTER 20

Patrick Miller and Keith Simon, "Truth over Tribe: Pledging Allegiance to the Lamb, not the Donkey or the Elephant"

I spent a lot of time reading philosophy in 2022, but the most interesting book I read that year was "Truth over Tribe". It is more of a political science book than a philosophy book, but I think philosophical thought is a pretty broad, encompassing genre. The book is co-authored by Patrick Miller and Keith Simon, both ministers at The Crossing (church) and hosts of the podcast "Truth over Tribe." The key point of the book is to unify the nation by releasing ourselves from polarized worldly ideology and coming together under the master of universal truth, Jesus. The following paragraph is not my own words. It is a series of direct quotations from throughout Miller and Simon's book, and they focus on some of the highlighted statements.

"Tribalism ruins your relationships... What if the goal wasn't to win an argument but to win a friend?.. I hope you're confident enough in what you believe to handle having your beliefs challenged and an open minded enough to change your mind if warranted... Do you want painful, pride-wrecked relationships with family and friends? Or do you want love powerful enough to outlast conflict created by names on a ballot?.. Tribalism makes you anxious... Fear and anxiety are not always proportional to actual risk... Nothing-not even abandonment by your own tribe can separate you from the love of God... Tribalism incentivizes *inauthenticity.* Will you be authentic even when it comes at a cost? God loves intellectual authenticity... God never coerces belief... Tribalism creates your enemies... We took the time to discover we all shared something greater in common: a desire to see our city flourish... Jesus founded the one and only tribe whose purpose is to put others first... Tribalism blinds you... Are your loves in the right order?.. Does your love for the Lamb transcend your love for the elephant or the love of the donkey?.. The more you assume the best about others, the more you can assume you're walking in God's grace... There are reasons why we are tribal beyond things we can say about each person's character... Your brain is tribal because of [hormones] and [neurons]... Survival outside of Eden conditioned human evolution to make all of us tribal... We're not the descendants of astronauts. We're the descendants of stone age survivors... Every living human is both a glory and a ruin... Facebook and Instagram feeds are tribal... Your phone isn't spying on you. It's guessing, and it knows so much about you, most of its guesses are correct... My personal responsibility is to be sober minded on the internet and to know Jesus commanded me not to be controlled by the world... Personal truth is tribal... When everything boils down to personal taste, truth loses flavor (Critical Theory). An entirely subjective truth, rooted only in the opinions of the tribe, not only makes culture wars inevitable, it makes them unresolvable (Conspiracy Theory)... Communities are tribal... You were designed by God to flourish in a robust, trusting, generous, self-giving network of relationships. Without it, you wither... If you want to be in a community full of diverse, crosscutting relationships, you'll need to think less of yourself and more of others... We must leave tribalism behind... Journey toward Eden... Why is the world not the way it's supposed to be? Artists, protestors, and politicians all have their answers. What's yours?.. Everyone wants the kingdom without the king because they want the kingdom on their own terms... We must show generosity and kindness... We have more in common than we realize... With so much in common, how can we be divided?..

Tribalism simply cannot withstand the weight of self-sacrificial generosity... Give time. Give encouragement. Give kindness... Would you pledge allegiance to Jesus?.. You must never allow your party's platform or interest to shape your ethics and beliefs more than Jesus's teachings do... It's a good sign to admit when you don't know... *Incompetence* breeds *confidence*... Don't believe everything you think... God designed you to have limits. He designed you to *not know*. He designed you to discover. To learn. To rethink. To explore... It helps to cross tribal lines... The line between good and evil didn't cut between parties. It cut through both parties... The idea of "us" and "them" is nothing new. You should feel more at home with people who share your faith than people who share your politics. Listen. One of the greatest gifts God can give you is a friend who sees the world differently than you. Don't let tribalism steal the joy of being wrong. Join an inclusive tribe. Jesus came to call a diverse, multi-ethnic, multi-lingual, multi-national group to follow Him. Following Jesus should lead us to form a worldwide tribe that welcomes everyone and charitably dialogues over our differences."

Granted, these bites of sentences do not build a very thorough story of the authors' full argument, but I hope there is something in there to intrigue you enough to get this book and give it a read. Without a doubt, it has the ability to redevelop the way you think about the self and how you fit into the world around you.

Patrick Miller and Keith Simon talk a lot about overcoming tribalism and ending division. Key points were admitting we don't actually know all things and getting out of the echo chamber. These things create isolation in the way we think and who we choose to interact with. It eliminates cognitive diversity, and creates polarity and divisiveness. Divisiveness is engrained in our human biology and is capitalized for profit on us by the institutions we live in. The media understands this and uses it for their profit. They sensationalize news stories and cause us to stereotype our opponents and those different than us. It causes us to think there is a problem with everyone who does not share the exact same beliefs with us, when really there is no problem with them. Social media and internet news feeds give us information that stimulates impulsive unity and impulsive division. Jesus knew how to combat this. He truly has the answers to all of life's mysteries. He said love your enemy no matter who they are or where they come from. Even each of his disciples were not from all the same demographics. They were all from different walks of life, fisherman, revolutionaries, tax collectors, etc. We are called to listen to other people, and listening to other people is the best way to gain wisdom. And at no point does any one person have all the right answers. Listening allows for cognitive diversity, diversity not defined by gender, ethnicity, or economic status. Listening to people who think the same as you locks you into echo chambers. Sure it feels good to be validated by those we share time and space with, but it does nothing to explore the truth or embody diversity. To avoid echo chambers and get more diversity in the world we should patiently listen to all people even if they have a drastically different perspective than ourselves. It is okay to admit we don't know and not knowing is by no means wrong. That helps us produce better ideas, identify problems earlier, serve more people, and make better decisions. First remove yourself from echo-chamber-groups. Second listen to those you might not agree with and keep an open mind in doing so. Tribalism is a hinderance to society (but feeds our impulsive desires). Choosing the way of Christ is the only true way to overcome this. The only way out of tribalism is to join a bigger, less specialized tribe, Jesus's tribe.

PART III

Concluding Thoughts

CHAPTER 21

Responsibilities to God

This two-part format cannot fully frame both of the objects of focus and drive home the point I set out to address and possibly resolve in this venture. The objective was to discover the intangibles that defuse tyranny. Defusing tyranny requires both application and theory. The first part of my endeavor, hiking Yellowstone and Glacier National Parks, reflects on the natural world God has created, and with it, communion with His Holy Spirit. The second part, analyzing philosophical thought about government, liberty and justice, reflects upon manmade institutions of society and the theories that premise such. Biblical truth is the link needed to connect the transcendental elements of nature with the logical elements of philosophy. It is a tough gap to bridge, but the two points have always laid adjacent to each other. Experience and logic are not all that far apart. A cup of coffee on a crisp mountain morning is a transcending experience and we can reason why. The beauty of the mountains drew us there to feel and reflect on the Spirit of the Creator. To rationalize the high you get standing by tall mountain peaks takes reflection. Universal truth is the link needed to bridge the gap. Reflection, logic, and ideas are used to describe our experiences and put them into perspective. The experience Kelly and I took on by taking a train across the country to hike Glacier and Yellowstone National Parks built a frame of relativity about our position in the world. As we reflected on biblical truth, we felt revelation, deep and obscure. God's consciousness and the habits of His energy are evident while tromping over the landscape and breathing in the mountain air. Describing the purpose for this world and the deep connection we feel to it leaves a gap when we go searching for reason. God is omnipresent. He is everywhere at all times. His energy and consciousness dwells in all things and spills onto us. With reverence for universal truth, we begin to fathom this with greater depth. There is much in this world we have not discovered, and much that exceeds the laws of nature. Miracles and the supernatural are more than we can comprehend with thoroughness. Trying to rationalize them might drive one nuts. We must have a foundation of universal truth when considering the supernatural and divine. We must see beyond this world and beyond ourselves.

We must admit *when* we do not know, and we must not believe everything we think. We were made to learn and discover. We were not made to know. Furthermore, finding belief in every impulsive thought that crosses our minds will lead us to stray from good judgement. The Bible has answers for those who search it. It might be the most supernatural book ever written. It holds inspiration, love, and reverence for God. It is the most widely read book in the world. If something has remained so popular yet so controversial for two millennia or more, there is no doubt that it holds a great deal of universal truth. The Bible's depiction of the beauty and supernatural forces within God leaves us in awe and wonder.

This work of mine is merely evidence upon which we can build a deeper relationship with the Creator and His creation. It is a platform or viewpoint from which we can approach God and approach people based in truth, compassion, and guidance. Without our relationship with God, everything on Earth exists in and of itself. There would be no deeper meaning. Reality would be merely superficial. So, to find a deeper meaning, I ask, what are emblems of freedom? Whatever they are, we must identify them and incorporate them into our lives to find restoration from the broken state the nation and the world is in. Elements holding universal truth have the power to restore peace, tranquility, strength, and prosperity. And to establish those things, we must regain a willingness to work and contribute to well-ordered society. Reflect on what we have to offer the world and the good we can do for the world. We must appoint leaders who are fair and honest. Their will and the will of God should be in alignment. We must build up from a foundation of universal truth. The truth will set you free. The first step is identifying truth. The second step is restoration.

The Old Testament said the government would rest on Christ's shoulders. Government ruled *by the people* was originated by the Jews in the time of Moses through their covenant with God. There was trust from the people that God would lead them in the right direction. If we turn to God and govern accordingly, society will be in a righteous state. It's not as much about the do's and don'ts of God but rather having a relationship with Him. He made promises and he kept them so long as their trust remained in Him. As time progressed and the many societies of history have evolved, humans have had the uncanny ability to deviate from God's plan. We push His values aside, and as a result our societies and communities crumble. It is strange to His character that God shows vengeance towards us here on Earth. We all wish he was a little quicker with retribution and kick the evil out of our world. When the masses are disobedient for long enough he sends a storm our way to get our attention and draw us back to Him. That is painful and not natural to the will of God. Love and compassion are more natural to God's character, but he will show wrath when people place idols before the Lord. When we violate this most fundamental commandment – keeping God first in our lives – it infuriates Him. He is a patient God, but patience is not infinite. God is divine and supernatural. Covenant society is an *institution of the divine and supernatural*. The power placed in our leaders does not require the guidance or approval of the Lord. People have developed societies and government to their own accord, apart from God, throughout time. Those societies seem to fall because of two reasons: 1) The thirst for power by those ruling, and 2) The impulsive desires embedded in the human flesh. The unjust will chase these things despite being displeasing to God. Fools pay no heed. American society was founded on a covenant with God, understanding that we had responsibilities to each other and responsibilities to the Almighty. By developing a government *of the people, by the people, and for the people,* each one of us is responsible for our own lives, part of that responsibility being our good standing with the Creator. It gave us liberty on a personal level, but it also gave us responsibility on a societal level. We have the liberty to adventure, but we must make sacrifices for the wellbeing of our communities. What could be accomplished was proportional to our accountability. When we hold ourselves accountable, the propensity for accomplishment increases.

CHAPTER 22

Limits on Liberty

Within the principles of government, liberty, and justice, there appears to be a spectrum of feasibility. There appears to be limits on things that are and are not possible. There appears to be limits to the levels of splendor that can be achieved by each individual within social unions. Placing your convictions too close to the fringe of those limits - the extremes - makes cooperating toward a common goal harder to achieve. A position of moderation assists sustainability of social programs; actually being able to produce goods and services in a way that is fair to everyone and actually obtainable. Officials representing pie-in-the-sky lifestyles exist on the fringe of what is realistic and honorable. We must examine ourselves and those representing us for values of freedom, namely stability and respect.

The principle of stability is necessary to sustain and perpetuate the good of society. Treasures of the wilderness are simple and the treasure we chase in our personal lives should be the same. They sustain by not sacrificing too much in the immediate sense. Rawls talked about stability in "A Theory of Justice" and stated that stability is most readily achieved when society is well ordered, and its statutes are publicly known. A premise of transparency assists citizens in observing the true intentions of our leaders and helps alert us to when changes should be made to our laws and procedures. Still, we must be prudent in the information we accept as truth. Rock solid evidence should not be perverted into a fallacy. There is much rhetoric to coerce us into a state of fear, and there is also no requirement for transparency among government officials. We should steel ourselves against the agendas of madmen, both traditional and progressive. We absolutely cannot live in a state of fear. Find confidence, faith, and admiration in the Almighty. Take heart and find hope that there is more to life than what we see in this world. Challenge yourself in the wilds, learning truth and virtue. Honesty and virtue are evidence of quality leaders. Transparency is a need of the people. Lack of honesty, transparency, and virtue is a huge injustice. It poses challenges towards growing respect and reduces stability.

CHAPTER 23

Generosity

The underlying cause of hate is division. What defeats hate is love. When we show generosity, we show love. When we show generosity, we show unity. Generosity is a principle that should be embraced for the sake of us all feeling loved and cared for. Sometimes we need help and generosity to maintain dignity. We should give a portion of what we have to others who are in need and cannot provide for themselves. Having basic necessities leads to a dignified life, a matter of self-respect and honor, and these are required by all, as Rawls puts it, to sustain justice and promote well-ordered society, a place where we can all thrive and express our nature as individuals in just ways. Satisfaction and appreciation will then grow in the hearts of the beloved. Feed the hungry and clothe the naked. We should expect generosity out of ourselves. Being selfless advocates supplying necessities to those who have less, little, or none. Putting ourselves *first* in all situations incorporates elements of greed into our character. It is mindless ignorance of the needs of others in the world. Experiencing nature will remind each of us that none of us are the center of the universe. If we find unity through generosity, we cut off the division that inspires hate.

Consistent generosity takes practice and commitment, and practicing generosity is not inherently progressive. Jesus claimed that feeding the hungry, nursing the sick, sheltering the homeless, and clothing the naked was a spiritual effort that extended beyond the beneficiaries out onto the heart of Christ. If you did this for the least of these, you did this for Him. Whether progressive or traditional, there are four things to always keep in mind when weighing justification for giving. First, there is no free lunch. Everything comes at the cost of something else, sacrifice. Time and energy are the fundamental elements that all other resources are dependent upon, so generosity with our resources requests sacrifices of our time and energy. Second, God always bats last. The Almighty will have the final say, so stingy or generous, we will all be judged. No matter what, if God wills it, nature can swallow us. Furthermore, allocations of blessings will always be passed from the hand of God. He will choose who to bless and who to smite, so being obedient is more likely to bestow the blessings that produce a fruitful world. Thirdly, making sacrifices is love in action. We do not want to part with our resources, but a compassionate heart will see the value in giving up a portion of what we have for the sake of another being better off. Fourthly, appreciating those sacrifices is respect in action. Gratitude and respect should always be given when someone helps. When we no longer respect, the beautiful bosom that once nourished is now the hand that punishes. Lack of appreciation causes the giver to feel violated and robbed, halting the flow of love, and usurping a resistance to ever give again.

Fear is the greatest inhibitor to progress. Refuse to live in fear, and be fearless with your generosity. When we work hard to make a difference in the lives of other people, there is a rewarding feeling felt within ourselves. Whether we want to admit it or not, governing officials of almost every nation on Earth have used fear to pressure our perspective and decision making. It causes division and dependency. It fuels hate. Refusing to live a life of fear is living at the heart of both faith and of liberty. And with liberty is freedom. And with freedom is generosity. We should not be divided by hate and fear. Fearless generosity and fearless compassion allocate dignity to those in dire need of it. Do not let the system intimidate you into fear, and do not let tribal impulses fuel division. Be content where you are right now. Do not be afraid of doing without. Thoreau said, "A man is rich in that which he can afford to do without." Emerson said, "In nature we return to faith and reason." Fear of missing out is the seed of greed and it drives us to be lavish with our consumption and wasteful with our resources. It perpetuates selfish lifestyles. If your eyes are open in nature, you are never missing out. It will compel us to share and manage our resources with discipline and not be wasteful. It feels good to give and it provides hope for the less fortunate. Be rewarded with the positive differences you make in the world. Also encourage those around you to be generous. When we feel the goodness of generosity, and set an example for others to follow, quality of life is improved, improved the most for those worst off. Each of us should be grateful for what we have been given and the beauty in the world around us. The power and means to help; the comfort and joy of a dignified existence.

Some wish to promote generosity and social programs for the wrong reasons and in the wrong way to break down traditional ways of life for the zest of something novel and progressive. Government has no right to give away money that was not theirs in the first place. Leaders should not change the way out of boredom, for the sake of changing the way, and thereby making a name for themselves. But if tradition shows righteousness by way of virtue, then why should tradition be attacked or destroyed? Not all traditions are righteous, but not all traditions require reformation to instill justice. Reformation should be generalized and subtle. That is the way the Almighty appears to work – subtle changes over time – so we should emulate the same methods. *Glamourous* lives will not be created for the poor by forced giving from the middle class. That does not mean the middle class as well as the upper class should not accommodate for the dignity of the poor. The upper class and the middle class should find a willingness in their hearts to give as they are able. It's okay to sacrifice some convenience and luxury for the wellbeing of those who have less, little, or none. Royalty will be humbled by recognizing how modestly the lower class survives. The upper class just might have to walk in the lower class's shoes to fully appreciate it. Any attempt to destroy the middle class and the working class, making them tools of the deep-state, should be transparently seen as an attempt to make the baseline living conditions of the whole nation even lower.

CHAPTER 24

Strength and Fearlessness

Inflation and a well-fare-state do not build strength. Destruction is not a path to prosperity. Fear is not a path to hope. We should not compulsively support frenzied rhetoric. There must be grounds upon which to hold confidence and not be swayed by the newness of an idea. When we know we are helping, and our efforts are showing positive results, we should all have confidence that everything will work out for the good. Conversely, when the system uses fear tactics to make you dependent on their programs, then demands you worship them instead of having faith in universal truths, the system has failed. Justice has not been served and liberty has been cancelled.

The progressive rhetoric has been advertised to maximize our liberty and satisfy desires. Among those liberties and desires is sexual freedom. Allowing us to act upon all our sensual fantasies eats away at the soul, making us weak and weakening well-ordered society. In this way, our character is conditioned to lose prudence and self-control. We are good at getting ourselves into trouble. As a liberty that has been allocated to satisfy our desires, sexual promiscuity has practically been encouraged by modern American society. It has been justified by hedonism. Sexual promiscuity has preceded the fall of every major society in history, Rome and Greece among them. American society is no different. Sex appeal has become an attribute of the liberties progressives have been advertising and it can come in many forms: perverted jokes, masturbation, provocative photos, pornography, grooming, sex abuse, adultery, sex outside of marriage.

Keeping God first above all other things is the first step in preventing these things, preventing the demise of a nation. Along with sports, gambling, and the entertainment industry, sexiness has been one of the greatest idols Americans have been putting before the importance of God. Resisting sexual immorality restores our psychology and character, building endurance, and strengthening the will of individuals, families, and communities. We are healthier in both mind and body by exercising prudence and self-control. Each one of us should understand this and admit that something needs to be done about our transgressions, at the very least on a personal level. Sex was intended for an exclusive relationship where there is commitment and trust. Innocence in sex is impossible outside the sanctity of marriage and an exclusive relationship. Marriage, too, takes self-discipline to honor. Marriage is necessary. Marriage offers security as it is an opportunity for you to give domain over your most intimate self to your spouse who you trust. It is one of the most underrated institutions of love and is disrespected because we are bad at seeing the bigger picture. In the institution of marriage, we are honoring a union of souls that are fused together and never meant to be separated and rematched. If our culture is quick and dirty, perverted, we have no ground to claim righteousness. We have no innocence, and we cannot hope for blessings. Preserving innocence displays obedience to the God of all love and this will bestow blessings from Him.

Every type of sexual immorality is disobedience to God, but I believe there are greater and lesser degrees of sexual immorality. I have been guilty of some of these wrongs as I believe most people have at one point or another in their lives. In fact, I think very few haven't. But this does not mean we should accommodate for the activities, nor give them high standing in our belief systems. We should turn from these things and practice prudence and self-control, drawing near to God. Not putting these lustful passions before the importance of God is paramount.

CHAPTER 25

Wrath and Guidance

Studying human history in the Bible, God's wrath always came when we put our idols before God. So, it's important to identify things that we might put higher value on than our attitude toward the Lord, and loving in the Spirit of Christ. If sensual pleasure comes before God, then what is to protect us from the wrath of God? Furthermore, our outlook on *making love* might need reconsidered if the idea of "making love" to the one we love is replaced with the idea of "F***ing" the ones we are loosely attracted to. This perspective reverses the forces that keep the world going round and leads us in a bad direction bound for doom. I pray we are prudent in our relationships and righteous in the things we put our faith in.

Christians behaving badly does not bring glory to God. A reverence for God and compassion towards all people is what brings glory to God. Losing yourself in the beauty of nature easily brings about this reverence. A cup of camp-coffee at dawn will teach you that God is compassionate yet wild. Duly, our responsibility is outlined in Bible verse Micah 6:8 "He has told you, human one, what is good and what the LORD requires from you: to do justice, embrace faithful love, and walk humbly with your God. (CEB)." Resisting immoral sexual behavior is a portion of what the Lord requires from you. Do justice. Embrace faithful love. And walk humbly with God. The calling might be easier if we were all the same, but we're not. God made us all different and still expects us all to get along and show love to each other. God wants to see love in action, not just passions of the flesh. Prejudice and discrimination are not any part of the love equation. As we see and feel differences among one another, we can get uncomfortable, uncomfortable with ourselves, and uncomfortable with those around us. Don't let the discomfort of our differences push us to reach for the low hanging fruit of discrimination. Discrimination is not an expression of love. Neither is it funny nor beneficial for any reason. Observing the differences in our appearance and behavior is all too easy and can lead to alienating people for no good reason. Love your neighbor just as you love yourself. Work in a way that everyone around you feels the love of God. The richness of diversity is embodied when we do not alienate people, communities, relationships, and social unions because of their appearances. Be inclusive and approach people with a humble heart. Be innocent and compassionate the way nature has taught us.

If we have a problem with the way someone is behaving, we do not need to shame them for honest mistakes or conditions they were born into. People are quick to judge when we should be quick to listen. With a little truth and insight, we can offer guidance. After you hear another's story, we can direct them down right paths should they be willing to listen. Listen first, and never discriminate. Sometimes it's the low road, the quick road, and the easy way to shame someone instead of working out problems and offering guidance. Instead of shaming, offer grace and forgiveness. Guiding others in the right direction is a responsibility of the community, but guidance is not needed for innocent differences. *Innocent* differences embody diversity. When there is a difference that crosses the line between ethical and unethical – honest and dishonest – offer direction instead shame. Placing individuals into a presumed class because their outward appearance or observable behavior is different puts them in a margin that robs a person of dignity and self-respect. In nature, we realize our equality. Ethical habits, like honesty, build dignity, character, and self-respect. These values build stronger unions, and our values determine the strength at which communities can withstand hardship. The more often we connect with our natural surroundings and meditate on God, the stronger our relationships will be.

If lying is an ideal that we adhere to as a means to exist, survive, and succeed how can there be hope for goodness and resilience from hardship? "Hard times make strong people, strong people make good times, good times make weak people, weak people make hard times" – Jonathan Davis. If dishonesty is our weakness how susceptible will we be towards hard times? How reliable will the domains, institutions, and industries we depend on be if our world cannot at its least be honest.

CHAPTER 26

Sacrifice and Self-discipline

Separating from vice takes the power of sacrifice and self-discipline. It takes the willpower to overcome temptation. It is more of a spiritual concept than a social one, but despite having predominantly spiritual qualities, sacrifice and self-discipline can reap great benefits in all aspects of our lives, approaching a means of atonement, reparations for our sins. With practice, denying ourselves can make stronger individuals and stronger communities. The general premise of self-discipline and atonement is to deprive ourselves of basic wants such as food, television, cell phones, internet, alcohol, marijuana, or tobacco, just to name a few, for a period of time without the direct intention of giving up the item permanently. We must suffer in privation to gain gratitude and condition our souls to navigate crises. It aids in breaking bad habits and reveals things about committing to self-control. Fasting, as it relates to food and eating, is the most historic version of such privation, but other habits that condition our perception can be given up for a short period of time in an attempt to recondition our internal faculties of sense and cognition. The amount of time these things can be forsaken can be two hours, two days, two weeks, or any amount of time sufficient to rewire the way we think, feel, and operate. Different stimuli send impulses through our nervous system conditioning the way we perceive and interact with the world around us. By depriving ourselves of a particular stimulus for a sustained period of time, our faculties have an opportunity to reboot, and start from zero. It is most valuable to the character of a person because this depravation gives our character time to grow and experience new things, live in a new way, or at the very least redirect where our habits were taking us. This also deprives stimuli of the opportunity to cripple us by our indulgences. There is no need for convictions of permanent abstinence in practicing atonement this way, just a hard and fast period sufficient to stress and recover, or "atone" the mind and body. The amount of time taken must be, at a minimum, stressful to whatever faculties are being deprived of the stimulus of choice. In stressful deprivation, temptation will set in. It is easy to start with gusto, but challenging to achieve real results, but through our suffering we show God gratitude and strength. This is where discipline and self-control come in. Self-restraint. Thus, a challenge. Our minds and bodies will crave and cry out for whatever is being deprived, but one must push through these stresses to achieve the beneficial effects. Mapping out sacrifice and self-discipline in writing could be advantageous. Reminding ourselves day in and day out what we are not to do, and remembering what day we will allow ourselves to return to the habit keeps the goal in focus and the path to success more achievable. Look at each day, hour, week as its own obstacle, saying "I will only worry about today, giving today my best." Or, "I will only worry about 12:00 pm – 2:00 pm, giving these two hours my best." Through temporary sacrifice and self-discipline, we reward ourselves with indulgences after taking the time to recondition our habits. This can rest and reset neuropathways, organ systems, or tissue. If you cannot return to the habit with moderation, it must be given up completely. Furthermore, habits that are completely immoral, like pornography, should not be acceptable in any amount. Even social media and television can abuse the mind, heart, and soul. Atoning against these indulgences can be powerful, too. When we return to the habit, it is important not to overindulge. You just took 2 days without flipping on the TV. Do not sit and binge-watch your favorite show from the time you get home from school or work until you go to bed. Replace bad habits with healthy ones. Try reading or meditating. They have tangential effects that postulate out through other parts of your life forming healthier habits in the greater scope of one's lifestyle. Set aside time for more controlled living.

Moderation is key in building healthy habits. It produces long-term benefits. Thoreau said, "A man is rich in that which he can afford to do without." If we limit our dependencies and take away the crutches, we will undoubtedly make stronger contributions in our lives. Show sacrifice and self-control enough to give rest and let the mind and body recharge. We must deny ourselves carnal pleasures. It's a challenge, but achieving anything you want in life takes sacrifices. Strength will build and improve the more you practice it. Righteousness parallels sacrifice, and in the name of improved harmony, we should consider the need to endure suffering.

CHAPTER 27

A Relationship with God

Respect and cooperation will get you further in life than wit or talent ever will. The true aim of tolerance is that we, with all our different views, will communicate peacefully. There is plenty of room in the world for humble people, but very little room in this world for arrogance. In order to be fair, to respect and cooperate, we, every one of us, must allow our ears to do more work than our mouths. Don't let the ego overrule our actions. Don't let expressions of wit and displays of talent override our desire to contribute to the greater good. Don't let the ego get in the way of solving problems. Just as we should remain humble with our resolve, we should also avoid blaming others for our problems. Foremost, always evaluate the problems within ourselves before placing blame on others. If others are honestly the problem, offer guidance instead of blame. Don't accuse. Accusations solve little to nothing. Our problem solving should be rooted in unbiased, impartial solutions. Our objectives and means to achieving them should be realistic and driven by the desire to do the right thing. Doing the right thing for the sake of doing the right thing produces excellence in the greater scope, even if it requires sacrifice or isn't in our own personal interest.

We should be generous with our time, talents, wealth, and love. And we should all work hard to make a contribution and earn a dignified living. Generosity and self-worth are not completely independent of each other. I appreciate what I earned for myself, and I feel good about giving back a little extra that I have. Hopefully it aids in giving someone else a more dignified life. Expecting out of ourselves reasonable sacrifices, monetary and otherwise, to help those in need is not socialism. Socialism is the embodiment of working to produce equal standards of living. Socialism that creates dependency on government programs is not the same as generosity. Generosity and socialism are not the same. Generosity is impartial. It is perfect procedural justice. Generosity is what Jesus taught. Giving is good, but enabling laziness and disrespect is bad. Expecting hard-working people to tighten their belts for the sake of those who refuse to put forth an effort behind a mask of apathy, dissent, or excuses does not promote a state of equality, and it definitely doesn't move a nation into better circumstances. It reduces both fairness and efficiency. Seizing the power from a nation of people and putting it in the hands of a few leaders cripples the authority of the people. On the other hand, denial of dignity supports a wildly depraved, despotical position, hardly coexistence. Totalitarianism and forced giving allow for no measure of self-esteem, or self-worth, and creates hostility. At one end of the effort-spectrum lies enabling. At the other end lies effort. Within that spectrum, we can promote productive bodies to add value to our communities through intrinsic, intangible treasures... attributes to our own character. Obtaining a sense of self-esteem without a sense of accomplishment is almost impossible, but by what means do we find a sense of accomplishment? Adventure and discovery can give a sense of accomplishment, but even greater, expressing our nature in ways that promote the success of a well-ordered society gives us a sense of accomplishment. All of this gives us satisfaction and vision of where we fit into the world.

Sacrifices of time, effort, and resources deserve compensation. Private property, though not deserving to be the primary reason for all our efforts, does have the ability to contribute to self-worth. Nice clothes, cool gear, a clean comfortable home, and a reliable vehicle – the ability to go – can make life feel more valuable. If we achieve these things by putting forth an honest effort toward a need within society, it can aid in the feeling of accomplishment. To promote justice, we must make available opportunities to earn a sense of accomplishment. Otherwise, the world we are in and the people around us will seem to have little purpose. We begin brooding over "what's in it for me." We begin devising plans on how to manipulate people for self-gain; injustice. The term "useful idiots' refers to the use of people for despotical purposes. These people are treated as tools only to be shown no gratitude or respect for their efforts. Don't give someone the power to manipulate you. We should reflect on the purpose of our efforts. Is the cause virtuous? Is it fair and realistic? Is it impartial? To assume, accuse, instigate, or be hostile should be seen as the evils they are, then removed. Better to be compassionate. Being flashy, competitive, loud, or profane for the sake of the ego has no quality of goodness. It opposes cooperation. We need to facilitate compassion, harmony, and stability, not fuel the ego. Stability takes self-control, committing to good deeds even when we feel otherwise. What can be said about the way we value commitment? What does that say about the people we are – the contributions we make to our communities – our hopes and expectations for the future of the world. Having a spirit of commitment enriches our social unions, giving us the power to persevere to good outcomes through the trials and tribulations.

When we develop a relationship with God, we submit to the greater good and gain identity and purpose. God makes us feel known and loved, and he prepares good works for us in His name. We gain self-esteem through a relationship with God. By carrying out the good works God has prepared for us, we feel identity and accomplishment. These good works will promote balance, harmony, and stability. Society cannot grow by egoism, manipulating others, or harboring a love of injustice. Instead, we must look to communal relationships with God for the whole of society to grow and advance towards righteousness and piety. Different people agreeing on the same means to achieve this is the hard part. We all must keep perspectives of universal truth.

Universal truth shows no favoritism. It is impartial and diverse. It takes focus and self-discipline from each of us. Universal truth is that we ought to expect fairness and honesty from everyone, including ourselves. We have all been made in the image of God's love and strength and that deserves respect. God created. Jesus is the Messiah. And we are all sinners. That's my summary of universal truth. Keep God in the heart, and a good heart-attitude towards God. With God, there is no limit to the goodness. But, our will and God's will must align. Conversely, keeping God out of your plans will always cause your plans to backfire. If socialism facilitates a godless society and calls us to be subservient to the state (as an eventuality instead of an initial circumstance) we remove autonomy and head towards a doomed fate. Socialism will aim to strip us of our property and belongings. If the government wants to rob these things from us, they are performing an injustice. Citizen controlled government where private property is one end of success, functions best when God is kept in the heart of citizens and governing officials.

God wants us to have an abundant life here on Earth. A relationship with God is not solely about being obedient to merit a comfortable afterlife. It's also about living a good life here on Earth. But it is done in whole populations as well as an individual-by-individual approach. When we can take satisfaction in the inner life we live, with all prudence and honesty, we will be righteous in God's eyes. Worshipping God is valuable. Worshiping the state and only being obedient to the directives of the state are sure to fail. There are limits on the quality of what human creatures can create. As creations of God, it is impossible for us to be greater than God. Humans have limits. God does not.

Obedience to God requires love and sacrifice, selflessness and generosity. We ought to be compensated for the sacrifices we make. Compensation for the effort and talent people put forth is fair and just. At least it ought to be. Fair compensation for an honest day's work is a cornerstone of well-ordered society.

We ought not be deprived of compensation by the oppression of the state. That has happened in communist countries in the past. In this way it is hard to build and maintain self-worth. It is a means to an aim of injustice. There are rewards beyond property and compensation for the sacrifices we make, though. Perpetuating the good is the greatest of those rewards. Rewards for sacrifice are a result of success and obedience. We should work for a successful "us" and an obedient "me" keeping the mind's eye ever watchful upon God. God influences by means of the Holy Spirit; miracles, natural phenomenon, love, and wrath. The supernatural forces of Christianity offer less mysticism and fantasy than other religious practices. Witchcraft, paganism, and animism have elements of fantasy and mysticism that enchant us in ways that Christianity usually does not. Still in the name of peace, abundance, and salvation I will place my faith in the Lord and in the Bible. The Bible is misunderstood by those who have read little or none of it. In there, too, are elements of mysticism. It just takes a little critical thinking. Spatial and temporal symbology build relationships between the believer and the savior that inhabit all elements of time and space. When studied specifically, symbology in the Bible has deeper meaning. Jesus came into the world at the time of the year just after the darkest day, the winter solstice, representing when light was becoming greater than darkness as daylight lengthened toward spring. He resurrected just after the spring equinox, when the length of daylight was now greater than the length of nighttime darkness, as earth broke the threshold of equal night and day. While on Earth, Jesus met with the spirits of Moses and Elijah, often referred to as the transfiguration of Christ. The spirit of Moses represented the fulfillment and spirit of the *law*, and the spirit of Elijah represented the fulfillment of the spirit of the *prophets*. Through Christ, the law and prophecy found in the Old Testament was fulfilled. There is plenty symbolism and display of awe and wonder in God's presence and timing. Read about Sampson or Daniel. There is an abundance of awe and wonder in the life, death, and resurrection of Christ Jesus. The miracles he performed in His life on Earth should be evidence enough that Jesus was God in the flesh. I mean he even raised a man from the dead! Even look to His punishment. God knew what it was like to suffer just the same as all humans. Jesus was God-in-the-flesh, and suffered death on the cross as well as the rest of the punishment of his conviction from the Pharisees and the Romans. This was all necessary for Jesus to ascend to Heaven and fulfill all prophecy about the Lord.

Truth from the Bible is being cancelled at a mind-boggling rate. No one wants to hear this story because it transports us away from sinful pleasures and self-centered dispositions, and shows us the pain we deserve, but Jesus took it on himself to reconcile us to God by suffering these things. Shamefully, we look for reasons to doubt God and put distance between us and Him. Many Christians blame Darwin for the reduction of the faithful, but Darwin is not to blame. Liberal sexual freedom and putting idols before God; sports, gambling, movie, music, are to blame. It just so happened that intellectual enlightenment was most prevalent in love-culture of the 1960's when the influence of Darwin's Theory of Natural Selection became popular. A similar thing happened with the Renaissance and the French Revolution. Lots of free thinking was experienced and the love generation got hijacked. All of a sudden, there are mechanics to creation, evolution, so that *must* mean God doesn't exist. What the hell is that!? An explanation of the mechanics of creation is no reason to doubt the existence of God. Reasons for doubt are faulty at best and uniformly sinful. When the culture sidesteps the reality of the supernatural and the almighty, we present excuses like evolution. Our short-sighted concept of truth and fallacy traps us. We are not greater than God. And because we have discovered the means by which natural phenomenon occurs does not make us omniscient nor give us supreme authority. It simply means we have pursued understanding. God wants us to pursue, discover, and understand, but we must understand to our deepest fiber that we are not all-powerful or all-knowing. Testimony and Christian literature can supplement the Bible to build interesting, dynamic, and personalized platforms of faith. Transcendentalism and rationale. Experience and theory. Let God's inspiration fill your heart. Let the Holy Spirit transform your mind. Specific insight can add depth to our appreciation of what it took to create our world. And, if we are going to accept evolution in a *biological* sense, then should we not also accept evolution in a *climatological* sense, too? Things change through time. That's a fact. The reason for change can be debated, but I don't think we can gather enough evidence to soundly prove the reasons why these changes happen. There are too many variables. Undoubtedly, having to restructure our coastal landscapes and recovering from severe natural disasters presents challenges, but changing geography and the extinction of species is nothing new. Are they good things? No, probably not. But, what are we willing to sacrifice? Would you be willing to sacrifice television in all of its forms to achieve less CO_2 in the air? Would you turn off your TV to reduce the amount of heat given off by the screen into the insulated atmosphere? Will we quit burning the energy to fuel lights in a football stadium, night club, or arena. Can we move away from disposable lifestyles? Can we distance ourselves from convenience and luxury? Are we willing to sacrifice sinful pleasures like gambling, whiskey, and pornography to be reshaped into a righteous existence? Will we quit believing we have all the answers and begin placing our trust in God's ways?

CHAPTER 28

Approaching the Bible

What is the purpose of the Bible, and what is its literature about? It is about God, His love, His wrath, and His people. It is about the beginning of human civilization and God's covenant with the Jews. It is about the prophecy of the coming Lord. It is a document of what Christ taught, primarily, to love our neighbors and love our God, trusting in His ways, being less anxious about our lives. It is about the life, death, and resurrection of Jesus. It also reveals items about Heaven, the path to Heaven, and the Lord's return. It teaches us about the character of God, and how to treat others. In these arenas, the Bible can teach us how to make the most of our time here on Earth while not being hedonists, yet yearning for compassion, wisdom, and discovery. Reading other contemporary Christian literature assists in understanding the Bible better and adds perspective to the faith. Among some literature I found helpful are "What is the Gospel" by Greg Gilbert, "The Prodigal God" by Tim Keller, "Gentle and Lowly" by Dane Ortlund, and "Before you open your Bible" by Matthew Smethurst.

To shed a little light from the Bible in a short and simple manner, let's take a look at Smethurst's book, "Before You Open Your Bible." The author encourages us to look at the Bible in a number of ways. The heart-posture while reading can condition the way the Word is received. We are to look at the Bible "Prayerfully: Incline my heart to your testimonies, and not to selfish gain (Psalms 119:36). Open my eyes that I might behold wonderous things out of your law (Psalms 119:18). Unite my heart to fear your name (Psalms 86:11). Satisfy us in the morning with your steadfast love (Psalms 90:14)." We are to be open-minded about the work God has done in our lives and the lives around us. We should revere creation and live in awe and wonder of God's works. We should have confidence in the steadfast love and strength of the Lord. Smethurst invites us to look at the Bible humbly. The Bible is proof that God speaks to us and loves us even though we are creatures and sinners. His heart is gentle and lowly. He encourages us to look at the Bible desperately. The Bible is not a snack. It is survival food that sustains us. Sometimes, God's word is the only thing that can get us through a situation. Studiously. Love God with all your mind to be a good theologian and to add depth to your worship and understanding of God. We, as humans, were created to discover. Great depth can be gathered from scripture when it is studied closely. Obediently. We obey God and his commands for our best interest because He designed us and knows what will bring us the greatest joy. We must rely on God's ways and not our own, for just as the heavens are higher than the earth, so are God's ways our higher than our own. Joyfully. The purpose of the Bible is to fill us with the joy that spills out of God's heart onto those he rescues. The love that fills the hearts of those who love God is a practically indescribable emotion. Joy is the only word that comes close. Expectantly. Everything in the Bible has the power to transform our lives and the lives around us. We need to have confidence that it can get the work done. There is nothing too great or too small for God to use to make the world we live in a better place through us. Communally. As steel sharpens steel, so one believer sharpens another with attributes like a Bible centered church, pastors, and elders. The community of faith and the presence of the Holy Spirit are the embodiment of Christ's presence on earth, despite being crucified nearly 2,000 years ago. Smethurst finishes by encouraging us to look at the Bible Christo-centrically. The entire Bible is based around Jesus Christ. The life of Jesus was the point of the whole thing. The Old Testament is about the journey of God's chosen people, and prophecy revealing the coming Lord. The New Testament is about the life Christ lived on Earth and His effect on the world. Smethurst's conclusion was that "The way we treat the word of God reveals the way we really think and feel about him."

It is important to keep a good heart attitude towards God and hold the message of the Bible with reverence. Reading scripture keeps us connected to age old teachings and the character of God, the Creator of the universe. Practices of the world outside of the church can hit us heavy and fast. If you are Christian, it should come as no surprise some of the practices inside the church hit the outside world hard and fast. Love everyone, because you are representing the body of Christ. Christians behaving badly brings no glory to God. For everyone, life can feel like a blur, confusion. The Bible helps us focus priorities. Placing our affairs before the eyes of God is our greatest responsibility in life. Lessons about transparency and commitment allow us to step out of the traffic of noise, ignore the distractions, and prioritizes our yeses. Be mindful of limitations as they relate to productive rest. Try to eliminate hurry. Simple living has its value. There is a lot of information in the Bible, so reading scripture, alone, can feel a little overwhelming. God still speaks through his people in written works today. Seek those out as well to find accurate application to biblical teaching in contemporary life.

CHAPTER 29

Emblems of Freedom

After all of this, have we come to any understanding as to what emblems of freedom are? Adventure and discovery appear to be major parts of that definition, the result of a nation that was founded and functions upon ethics, justice, and universal truth. A lot hinges on those three things, namely honesty and fairness. Without ethics, justice, and universal truth, most of the comforts and joys the American people know today would be lost. Communion with other people, the self, and nature draw us into ideas of adventure and discovery. And the idea of self-expression cannot be forgotten in a free state, either. Those things require patience, and patience is the forefather of tolerance. Tolerance's primary goal is to communicate with those who are different than us in a peaceful way. Tolerance facilitates things like peace and understanding as they are important to progress, but tolerance and understanding are not the same things as approval of bad behavior. Understanding is more of a notion of empathy. Approval of bad conduct eats away at the stability of the self, the community, and the nation. It eats away at the fabric of clear reflection and engagement with the world God has placed us in. The whole world needs the freedom to engage and reflect. Reflecting on reality, supernatural forces being part of that, allows us to get a bearing on where we are right now, where we would like to be, and how to get there from here. Brooding over things or being glued to sensational coverage of current events is not impartial, unbiased reflection. Being brainwashed by the institutions of the world is crippling, and we should not allow them into our belief system. Tradition and well-ordered society have become the subject of ridicule because we have not lived out what Jesus and the Bible really taught: keep God first in everything and love your neighbor as you would love yourself. Admittedly, those things take sacrifice and discipline, things we don't like. But to be truly free, we must not be shackled by worldly desires and indulgences.

Good living has become so common in America and remained so for so long that we have become complacent about our spiritual lives. In our complacency the desire for shock-factor and strange and new perverted ways have been supported by bureaucrats and activists. Tradition and well-ordered society seem almost taboo to talk about in an endearing way. We have become familiar with the flaws of tradition and have become apt to wage war on them. Nevertheless, traditions have provided much stability in our lives. They have also created opportunities for those who pursue rich living, both worldly and sentimental. Do we work hard to sustain a reliable system where all who are willing to work can make a good life for themselves? The opportunity to make a good living through the willingness to work is not something that should be denied of the American people, especially because of the need of those not willing to work also needing to fare well. Success and stability give us less worry. An unpredictable world causes anxiety. When we are always amending laws or changing what is acceptable, we are undermining stability. Boredom and confusion are no one's friend. But how do we balance stability and renewal of the world? What pace and extent should renewal flow upon? Might standards of honesty and fairness, transparency and commitment, be the cornerstones of renewal? Stability and moderation prove beneficial more times than not. Is stability political ideology, or a principle of virtue?

The political ideology we identify with is less important than being a goodhearted person. Be fair and honest, and have a positive heart attitude towards God. Patience, gentleness, and gratitude. Love, compassion, and altruism should be where all change begins. It starts with self, so we must examine ourselves first. "You must all be quick to listen, slow to speak, and slow to get angry. (James 1:19 NLT)" Take a little time to discover. Solve problems where there are problems to solve. Admit when you don't know things. Few things are more important than keeping a clean home, cooking good meals, being a loving spouse, and a good role model to your children. We can readily be judged by the relationships we keep. Beyond that stay open to adventure and discovery. Incorporate ethics, justice, and universal truth into your daily lives, and have the courage to step outside of your comfort zone to feel, renew, and connect.

www.ingramcontent.com/pod-product-compliance
Lightning Source LLC
Chambersburg PA
CBHW020244130626
46549CB00005B/2052